GREATEST EVER
Pasta

p

This is a Parragon Publishing Book
This edition published in 2003

Parragon Publishing
Queen Street House
4 Queen Street
Bath BA1 1HE, UK

ISBN: 0-75259-091-X

Printed in Dubai

Produced by The Bridgewater Book Company Ltd

NOTE

Cup measurements in this book are for American cups. This book also uses
imperial and metric measurements. Follow the same units of measurement
throughout; do not mix imperial and metric.
All spoon measurements are level: teaspoons are assumed to be 5 ml and
tablespoons are assumed to be 15 ml. Unless otherwise stated, milk is assumed
to be whole milk, eggs and individual vegetables such as potatoes are medium,
and pepper is freshly ground black pepper.

The times given for each recipe are an approximate guide only because the
preparation times may differ according to the techniques used by different
people and the cooking times may vary as a result of the type of oven used.

Recipes using raw or very lightly cooked eggs should be
avoided by infants, the elderly, pregnant women, convalescents, and anyone
suffering from an illness.

Contents

Introduction

Pasta has existed in one form or another since the days of the Roman Empire and remains one of the most versatile ingredients in the kitchen. It can be combined with almost anything from meat to fish, vegetables to fruit, and is even delicious served with simple herb  sauces. No pantry should be without a supply of dried pasta, which, combined with a few other stock ingredients, can be turned into a mouthwatering and nutritious meal within minutes.

Most pasta is made from durum wheat flour and contains protein and carbohydrates. It is a good source of slow-release energy and has the additional advantage of being value for money. There is an enormous range of different types of pasta. Many are available both dried and fresh. Unless you have access to a good Italian delicatessen, it is probably not worth buying fresh unfilled pasta, but even supermarkets sell high-quality tortellini, capelletti, ravioli, and agnolotti.

Best of all, make fresh pasta at home. It is quite easy and worth the effort. You can mix the dough by hand or in a food processor.

Pasta Shapes

There are thought to be at least 200 different shapes of pasta with over 600 different names. New varieties are being designed constantly, and also the same shape may have different names in different regions of Italy. Basically, pasta falls into four categories: long round, long ribbons, tubes, and small shapes. Pasta may also be stuffed with a variety of fillings. The following is a list of some of the most frequently used types of unfilled pasta.

Cravatte, Cravattini bows

Cresti Di Gallo "cock's comb," curved shapes

Dischi Volante "flying saucers"

Ditali, Ditalini "little thimbles," short tubes

Eliche loose, spiral shapes

Elicoidali short, ridge tubes

Farfalle bows

Fedeli, Fedelini fine tubes twisted into skeins

Festonati short lengths, like festoons

Fettuccine narrow ribbon pasta

Fiochette, Fiochelli small bows

Frezine broad, flat ribbons

Fusilli spindles or short spirals

Fusilli Bucati thin spirals, like springs

Gemelli, "twins," two pieces wrapped together

Gramigna meaning "grass" or "weed," look like sprouting seeds from Emilia Romagna

Lasagna flat, rectangular sheets

Linguine long, flat ribbons

Lumache smooth, snail-like shells

Lumachine U-shaped flat pasta

Macaroni, Maccheroni long or short-cut tubes, may be ridged or elbow-shaped

Maltagliati triangular

Orecchiette ear-shaped

Orzi tiny, rice-like grains

Pappardelle widest ribbons, straight with sawtooth edges

Pearlini tiny discs

Penne quills, short, thick tubes with diagonally cut ends

Pipe Rigate ridged, curved pipe shapes

Rigatoni thick, ridged tubes

Rotelle wheels

Ruote wheels

Semini seed shapes

Spaghetti fine, medium, and thick rods

Spirale two rods twisted into spirals

Strozzapreti "priest strangler," double twisted strands

Tagliarini flat ribbons, thinner than tagliatelle

Tagliatelle broad, flat ribbons

Tortiglione thin, twisted tubes

Vermicelli fine, slender strands usually twisted into skeins

Ziti Tagliati short, thick tubes

Basic Recipes

Fresh Chicken Bouillon

MAKES 7½ CUPS

2 lb 4 oz/1 kg chicken, skinned

2 celery stalks

1 onion

2 carrots

1 garlic clove

few fresh parsley sprigs

9 cups water

salt and pepper

1 Put all the ingredients into a large pan and bring to a boil over a medium heat.

2 Using a slotted spoon, skim away any scum on the surface. Reduce the heat to a gentle simmer, partially cover, and cook for 2 hours. Let cool.

3 Line a strainer with clean cheesecloth and put over a large pitcher or bowl. Pour the bouillon through the strainer. The cooked chicken can be used in another recipe. Discard the other solids. Cover the bouillon and chill in the refrigerator.

4 Skim away any fat that forms before using. Store in the refrigerator for 3–4 days, until required, or freeze in small batches.

Fresh Vegetable Bouillon

This can be kept chilled for up to 3 days or frozen for up to 3 months. Salt is not added when cooking the bouillon: it is better to season it according to the dish in which it is to be used.

MAKES 6¼ CUPS

9 oz/250 g shallots

1 large carrot, diced

1 celery stalk, chopped

½ fennel bulb

1 garlic clove

1 bay leaf

few fresh parsley and tarragon sprigs

8¾ cups water

pepper

1 Put all the ingredients into a large pan and bring to a boil over a medium heat.

2 Using a slotted spoon, skim away any scum on the surface. Reduce the heat, partially cover and cook gently for 45 minutes. Let cool.

3 Line a strainer with clean cheesecloth and put over a large pitcher or bowl. Pour the bouillon through the strainer. Discard the herbs and vegetables.

4 Cover and store in small quantities in the refrigerator for up to 3 days.

Fresh Lamb Bouillon

MAKES 7½ CUPS

about 2 lb 4 oz/1 kg bones from a
  cooked joint or raw chopped
  lamb bones
2 onions, studded with 6 cloves, or
  sliced or chopped coarsely
2 carrots, sliced
1 leek, sliced
1–2 celery stalks, sliced
1 bouquet garni
about 2 quarts water

1 Chop or break up the bones and put into a large pan with the other ingredients and bring to a boil over a medium heat.

2 Using a slotted spoon, skin away any scum on the surface. Reduce the heat, partially cover and cook gently for 3–4 hours. Strain the bouillon and let cool.

3 Remove any fat from the surface and chill in the refrigerator. If stored for more than 24 hours the bouillon must be boiled every day, cooled quickly and chilled again. The bouillon may be frozen for up to 2 months; put into a large plastic bag and seal, leaving at least 1 inch/2.5 cm of headspace to allow for expansion.

Fresh Fish Bouillon

MAKES 7½ CUPS

1 head of a cod or salmon, etc. plus
  the trimmings, skin and bones or
  just the trimmings, skin and bones
1–2 onions, sliced
1 carrot, sliced
1–2 celery stalks, sliced
good squeeze of lemon juice
1 bouquet garni or 2 bay leaves

1 Wash the fish head and trimmings and put into a large pan. Cover with water and bring to a boil over a medium heat.

2 Using a slotted spoon, skim away any scum on the surface, then add the remaining ingredients. Cover and cook for 30 minutes.

3 Strain and let cool. Store in the refrigerator and use within 2 days.

Italian Cheese Sauce

Melt 2 tbsp of butter in a pan and stir in ¼ cup all-purpose flour until crumbly. Stir in 1¼ cups hot milk until thick and smooth. Add a pinch of nutmeg, dried thyme, 2 tbsp white wine vinegar, and season to taste with salt and pepper. Stir in 3 tbsp of heavy cream, ½ cup each freshly grated mozzarella and Parmesan cheeses, 1 tsp English mustard and 2 tsp of sour cream. Mix together thoroughly.

Soups

Soups are an important part of the Italian cuisine. They vary in consistency from light and delicate to hearty main meal soups. Texture is always apparent—Italians rarely serve smooth soups. Some may be partially pureed, but the identity of the ingredients is never entirely obliterated. There are regional characteristics too. In the north, soups are often based on rice, while in Tuscany, thick bean- or bread-based soups are popular. Tomato, garlic, and pasta soups are typical of the south. Minestrone is known worldwide, but the best-known version probably comes from Milan. However, all varieties are full of vegetables and are delicious and satisfying. Fish soups also abound in one guise or another, and most of these are village specialities, so the variety is unlimited and always tasty.

minestrone soup

serves eight–ten

3 garlic cloves

3 large onions

2 celery stalks

2 large carrots

2 large potatoes

¾ cup green beans

3½ oz/100 g zucchini

4 tbsp butter

¼ cup olive oil

2 oz/55 g rindless fatty bacon,
   diced finely

6⅞ cups vegetable or
   chicken bouillon

1 bunch fresh basil, chopped finely

⅜ cup chopped tomatoes

2 tbsp tomato paste

3½ oz/100 g fresh Parmesan
   cheese peel

¼ cup dried spaghetti, broken up

salt and pepper

freshly grated Parmesan cheese,
   to serve

1 Finely chop the garlic, onions, celery stalks, carrots, potatoes, beans, and zucchini with a sharp knife.

2 Heat the butter and oil together in a large pan over a medium heat. Add the bacon and cook for 2 minutes. Add the garlic and onion, and cook for 2 minutes. Stir in the celery, carrots, and potatoes and cook for 2 minutes.

3 Add the chopped beans to the pan and cook for 2 minutes. Stir in the zucchini and cook for an additional 2 minutes. Cover the pan and cook all the vegetables, stirring frequently, for 15 minutes.

4 Add the bouillon, basil, tomatoes, tomato paste, and cheese peel and season to taste. Bring to a boil, then reduce the heat and simmer for 1 hour. Remove the cheese peel and discard.

5 Add the pasta to the pan and cook for 20 minutes.

6 Ladle the soup into warmed soup bowls, sprinkle with freshly grated Parmesan cheese and serve.

COOK'S TIP

There are almost as many recipes for minestrone as there are cooks in Italy! You can add almost any vegetables you like and canned beans, such as lima beans.

bean & pasta soup

serves four

1⅓ cups dried navy beans, soaked,
   drained, and rinsed

4 tbsp olive oil

2 large onions, sliced

3 garlic cloves, chopped

14 oz/400 g canned
   chopped tomatoes

1 tsp dried oregano

1 tsp tomato paste

3 cups water

¾ cup small dried pasta shapes

4½ oz/125 g sun-dried tomatoes,
   drained and sliced thinly

1 tbsp chopped cilantro or
   Italian parsley

2 tbsp freshly grated
   Parmesan cheese

salt and pepper

1 Put the beans into a pan, cover with water, and bring to a boil. Boil rapidly for 10 minutes to remove any toxins, then drain and rinse.

2 Heat the oil in a large pan over a medium heat. Add the onions and cook until they are just starting to change color. Stir in the garlic and cook for 1 additional minute. Stir in the chopped tomatoes, oregano, and the tomato paste and pour over the water.

3 Add the cooked, drained beans to the mixture in the pan, bring to a boil and cover. Simmer for about 45 minutes, or until the beans are almost tender.

4 Add the pasta, season to taste with salt and pepper, and stir in the sun-dried tomatoes. Return the soup to a boil, partially cover and continue cooking for 10 minutes, or until the pasta is nearly tender.

5 Stir in the chopped cilantro or parsley. Taste the soup and adjust the seasoning, if necessary. Ladle the soup into 4 warmed soup bowls, sprinkle with freshly grated Parmesan cheese and serve immediately.

potato & parsley soup with pesto

serves four

3 slices rindless, smoked
   fatty bacon

1 lb/450 g mealy potatoes

1 lb/450 g onions

2 tbsp butter

2½ cups chicken bouillon

2½ cups milk

¾ cup dried conchigliette

⅝ cup heavy cream

1 tbsp chopped fresh parsley

salt and pepper

PESTO SAUCE

1 cup finely chopped fresh parsley

2 garlic cloves, minced

⅔ cup pine nuts, minced

2 tbsp chopped fresh basil leaves

⅔ cup freshly grated
   Parmesan cheese

white pepper

⅝ cup olive oil

TO SERVE

freshly grated Parmesan cheese

garlic bread

1 To make the pesto sauce, put all the ingredients into a blender or food processor and process for 2 minutes, or blend by hand.

2 Chop the bacon, potatoes, and onions. Put the bacon into a pan and cook over a medium heat for 4 minutes. Add the butter, potatoes, and onions and cook for 12 minutes.

3 Add the bouillon and milk to the pan, then bring to a boil and cook for 10 minutes. Add the pasta and cook for 12–14 minutes.

4 Blend in the cream and simmer for 5 minutes. Add the parsley and 2 tablespoons of pesto sauce. Ladle the soup into bowls and serve with the remaining pesto sauce, Parmesan cheese, and garlic bread.

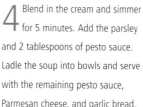

italian fish soup

serves four

4 tbsp butter

1 lb/450 g assorted fish fillets, such
   as sea bass and red snapper

1 lb/450 g prepared seafood, such
   as squid and shrimp

8 oz/225 g fresh crab meat

1 large onion, sliced

¼ cup all-purpose flour

5 cups fish bouillon

¾ cup dried pasta shapes, such as
   ditalini or elbow macaroni

1 tbsp anchovy paste

grated peel and juice of 1 orange

¼ cup dry sherry

1¼ cups heavy cream

salt and pepper

grated orange peel, to garnish

3 Gradually add the fish bouillon,
   stirring constantly, until the soup
comes to a boil. Reduce the heat and
simmer for 30 minutes.

4 Add the dried pasta shapes to the
   pan and cook for an additional
10 minutes.

5 Stir in the anchovy paste, orange
   peel, orange juice, sherry, and
the cream. Season to taste with salt
and pepper.

6 Heat until completely warmed
   through. Ladle the soup into a
warmed tureen or to 4 warmed soup
bowls and garnish with some grated
orange peel. Serve immediately.

1 Melt the butter in a large pan
   over a low heat. Add the fish
fillets, seafood, crab meat, and onion
and cook gently for 6 minutes.

2 Add the flour to the mixture,
   stirring carefully with a wooden
spoon to avoid any lumps.

chicken soup with stars

2 lb 12 oz/1.25 kg chicken pieces,
  such as wings or legs

2 quarts water

1 celery stalk, sliced

1 large carrot, sliced

1 onion, sliced

1 leek, sliced

2 garlic cloves, minced

8 peppercorns

4 allspice berries

3–4 fresh parsley stems

2–3 fresh thyme sprigs

1 bay leaf

¾ cup small dried pasta stars, or
  other very small shapes

chopped fresh parsley

salt and pepper

1 Put the chicken into a large flameproof casserole dish with the water, celery, carrot, onion, leek, garlic, peppercorns, allspice, herbs, and ½ teaspoon of salt. Bring just to a boil over a medium heat and skim off the foam that rises to the surface. Reduce the heat, partially cover, and simmer for 2 hours.

2 Remove the chicken from the casserole dish and let cool. Continue simmering the liquid, uncovered, for 30 minutes. When the chicken is cool enough to handle, remove the meat from the bones and, if necessary, cut into bite-size pieces.

3 Strain the liquid through a strainer and remove as much fat as possible. Discard the vegetables and flavorings. (There should be about 7½ cups of liquid.)

4 Bring the liquid to a boil in a clean pan over a medium heat. Add the pasta and reduce the heat so the liquid boils very gently. Cook for about 10 minutes, or until the pasta is tender, but still firm to the bite.

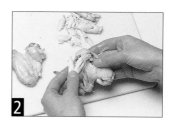

5 Stir in the chicken. Taste the soup and adjust the seasoning, if necessary. Ladle into warmed bowls, sprinkle with parsley and serve.

shrimp dumpling soup

serves four

DUMPLINGS

1⅝ cups all-purpose flour

¼ cup boiling water

⅛ cup cold water

1½ tsp vegetable oil

FILLING

½ cup ground pork

½ cup cooked, peeled
   shrimp, chopped

1¾ oz/50 g canned water chestnuts,
   drained, rinsed, and chopped

1 celery stalk, chopped

1 tsp cornstarch

1 tbsp sesame oil

1 tbsp light soy sauce

SOUP

3¾ cups fish bouillon

1¾ oz/50 g cellophane noodles

1 tbsp dry sherry

snipped fresh chives, to garnish

1 To make the dumplings, mix the flour, boiling water, cold water, and oil together in a bowl until a pliable dough is formed.

2 Knead the dough on a lightly floured counter for about 5 minutes. Cut the dough into 16 equal-sized pieces.

3 Roll the dough pieces into rounds about 3 inches/7.5 cm in diameter.

4 Mix all the filling ingredients together in a large bowl.

5 Spoon a little of the filling mixture into the center of each round. Bring the edges of the dough together, scrunching them up to form a "moneybag" shape. Twist to seal.

6 Pour the bouillon into a pan and bring to a boil over a low heat.

7 Add the noodles, dumplings, and sherry to the pan and cook for 4–5 minutes, or until the noodles and dumplings are tender. Ladle the soup into 4 large, warmed soup bowls, garnish with snipped chives and serve.

vermicelli & vegetable soup

serves four

1 small eggplant

2 large tomatoes

1 potato, peeled

1 carrot, peeled

1 leek

14½ oz/420 g canned
   cannellini beans

3¾ cups hot vegetable or
   chicken bouillon

2 tsp dried basil

½ oz/15 g dried porcini mushrooms,
   soaked for 20 minutes in enough
   almost boiling water to cover

¼ cup dried vermicelli

3 tbsp Pesto (see page 13)

freshly grated Parmesan cheese, to
   serve (optional)

1 Slice the eggplant into rings,
  about ½-inch/1-cm thick, then cut
each ring into 4 pieces.

2 Cut the tomatoes and potato into
  small dice. Cut the carrot into
sticks, about 1-inch/2.5-cm long and
cut the leek into rings.

3 Put the beans and their liquid in a
  pan. Add the eggplant, tomatoes,
potatoes, carrot, and leek, then stir.

4 Add the bouillon to the pan and
  bring to a boil over a medium
heat. Reduce the heat and simmer for
15 minutes.

5 Add the basil, dried mushrooms,
  their soaking liquid, and the
vermicelli and cook for 5 minutes.

6 Remove the pan from the heat and
  stir in the Pesto (see page 13).

7 Ladle the soup into 4 large,
  warmed soup bowls and serve
with Parmesan cheese (if using).

noodle soup

serves four

3 slices smoked, rindless fatty
    bacon, diced

1 large onion, chopped

1 tbsp butter

2½ cups dried peas, soaked in cold
    water for 2 hours and drained

10 cups chicken bouillon

8 oz/225 g dried egg noodles

⅝ cup heavy cream

salt and pepper

chopped fresh parsley, to garnish

Parmesan cheese croutons (see
    Cook's Tip), to serve

1 Put the bacon, onion, and butter
into a large pan and cook over a
low heat for about 6 minutes.

2 Add the peas and chicken
bouillon to the pan and bring to a
boil over a medium heat. Season
lightly with salt and pepper, then cover
and simmer for 1½ hours.

COOK'S TIP

To make Parmesan cheese
croutons, cut a French stick into
slices. Coat each slice with olive
oil and sprinkle with Parmesan
cheese. Cook under a preheated
hot broiler for about 30 seconds.

3 Add the egg noodles to the pan
and simmer for an additional
15 minutes.

4 Pour in the cream and mix
thoroughly. Ladle the soup into a
large, warmed tureen, garnish with
chopped parsley and top with the
Parmesan cheese croutons (see
Cook's Tip). Serve immediately.

minestrone with pesto

serves six

1 cup dried cannellini beans,
   soaked overnight

2 quarts water or vegetable bouillon

1 large onion, chopped

1 leek, trimmed and sliced thinly

2 celery stalks, sliced very thinly

2 carrots, chopped

3 tbsp olive oil

2 tomatoes, peeled and
   chopped coarsely

1 zucchini, trimmed and sliced thinly

2 potatoes, diced

¾ cup dried elbow macaroni, or
   other small macaroni

salt and pepper

4–6 tbsp freshly grated Parmesan
   cheese, to serve

PESTO

2 tbsp pine nuts

5 tbsp olive oil

2 bunches fresh basil,
   stems removed

4–6 garlic cloves, minced

¾ cup freshly grated romano or
   Parmesan cheese

1 Drain the beans, rinse, and put into a pan with the water or bouillon (avoid using a salty bouillon, or the beans will become tough during cooking.) Bring to a boil over a low heat, cover, and simmer for 1 hour.

2 Add the onion, leek, celery, carrots, and oil. Cover and simmer for 4–5 minutes.

3 Add the tomatoes, zucchini, potatoes, and macaroni Season to taste with salt and pepper. Cover again and continue to simmer for about 30 minutes, or until very tender.

4 To make the pesto, heat 1 tablespoon of the oil in a pan over a low heat. Add the pine nuts and cook until pale brown, then drain. Put the basil, nuts, and garlic into a food processor or blender and process until finely chopped. Alternatively, chop the basil finely by hand in a mortar and pound with the minced garlic with a pestle. Gradually add the remaining oil until smooth. Transfer to a bowl, add the cheese and season to taste. Mix.

5 Add 1½ tablespoons of the pesto to the soup and stir until well blended. Simmer the soup for an additional 5 minutes and adjust the seasoning, if necessary. Ladle the soup into 6 large, warmed bowls, sprinkle with the freshly grated Parmesan cheese (if using) and serve with the remaining pesto.

minestrade lentiche

serves four

4 strips sliced bacon, cut into
    small squares

1 onion, chopped

2 garlic cloves, minced

2 celery stalks, chopped

¼ cup dried farfalline or spaghetti
    broken into small pieces

14½ oz/420 g canned brown
    lentils, drained

5 cups hot ham or
    vegetable bouillon

2 tbsp chopped fresh mint

4 fresh mint sprigs, to garnish

1 Put the bacon into a large skillet together with the onions, garlic, and celery. Dry-fry for 4–5 minutes, stirring, until the onion is tender and the bacon is just starting to brown.

2 Add the pasta pieces to the skillet and cook, stirring constantly, for about 1 minute to coat the pasta thoroughly in the oil.

3 Add the lentils and bouillon and bring to a boil over a medium heat, then reduce the heat and simmer until the pasta is done.

4 Remove the skillet from the heat and stir in the chopped mint.

5 Ladle the soup into 4 warmed soup bowls and garnish with mint sprigs. Serve immediately.

VARIATION
Any type of pasta can be used in this recipe—try fusilli, conchiglie, or rigatoni, if you prefer.

COOK'S TIP
If you prefer to use dried lentils, add the bouillon before the pasta and cook for 1–1¼ hours, until the lentils are tender. Add the pasta and cook for an additional 12–15 minutes.

chicken & bean soup

serves four

2 tbsp butter

3 scallions, chopped

2 garlic cloves, minced

1 fresh marjoram sprig, chopped finely

12 oz/350 g boned chicken
   breasts, diced

5 cups chicken bouillon

12 oz/350 g canned garbanzo
   beans, drained

1 bouquet garni sachet

1 red bell pepper, diced

1 green bell pepper, diced

1 cup small dried pasta shapes,
   such as elbow macaroni

salt and white pepper

croutons, to serve

1 Melt the butter in a large pan over a medium heat. Add the scallions, garlic, marjoram, and diced chicken and cook, stirring frequently, for 5 minutes.

2 Add the chicken bouillon, garbanzo beans, and bouquet garni sachet, then season to taste with salt and white pepper.

3 Bring the soup to a boil over a medium heat, then reduce the heat and simmer for about 2 hours.

4 Add the diced bell peppers and pasta shapes to the pan, then simmer for an additional 20 minutes.

5 Ladle the soup into 4 warmed soup bowls and garnish with croutons. Serve immediately.

chicken ravioli in tarragon broth

serves six

8 cups chicken bouillon

2 tbsp finely chopped fresh
tarragon leaves

freshly grated Parmesan cheese,
to serve

HOMEMADE PASTA DOUGH

1 cup pasta or white bread flour,
plus extra if needed

2 tbsp fresh tarragon leaves, with
stems removed

1 egg

1 egg, separated

1 tsp extra virgin olive oil

2–3 tbsp water

FILLING

7 oz/200 g cooked chicken,
chopped coarsely

½ tsp grated lemon peel

2 tbsp chopped mixed fresh
tarragon, chives, and parsley

4 tbsp whipping cream

salt and pepper

1 To make the pasta, mix the flour, tarragon, and salt into a food processor and mix together. Beat the egg, egg yolk, oil, and 2 tablespoons of the water together. With the machine still running, pour in the egg mixture and process until it forms a ball, leaving the sides of the bowl virtually clean. If the dough is crumbly, add the remaining water. If the dough is sticky, add 1–2 tablespoons of flour and continue kneading in the food processor until a ball forms. Wrap and chill in the refrigerator for 30 minutes. Set aside the egg white.

2 To make the filling, put the chicken, lemon peel, and mixed herbs into a food processor and season to taste with salt and pepper. Chop finely, by pulsing. Scrape into a bowl and stir in the cream. Taste and adjust the seasoning, if necessary.

3 Divide the pasta dough in half. Cover one half with a damp dish towel and roll the other half on a floured counter as thinly as possible, less than ¹⁄₁₆ inch/1.5 mm. Cut out rectangles 4 x 2 inches/10 x 5 cm.

4 Put rounded teaspoons of filling on one half of the dough pieces. Brush around the edges with the egg white and fold in half. Press the edges gently but firmly to seal. Arrange the ravioli in one layer on a cookie sheet, dusted generously with flour. Repeat with remaining dough. Let the ravioli dry in a cool place for 15 minutes, or chill in the refrigerator for 1–2 hours.

5 Bring a large pan of lightly salted water to a boil over a medium heat. Drop in half the ravioli and cook for 4–6 minutes, or until done. Drain the ravioli on a clean dish cloth while cooking the remainder.

6 Meanwhile, put the bouillon and tarragon in a large pan, then bring to a boil over a medium heat. Reduce the heat to bubble very gently. Cover and simmer for 15 minutes, to infuse. Add the cooked ravioli to the bouillon and simmer for 5 minutes until heated through. Ladle into 6 large, warmed soup bowls and serve immediately with Parmesan cheese.

avgolemono

1 Pour the bouillon into a large pan and bring to a boil over a medium heat. Add the orzo and cook for 8–10 minutes, or until the pasta is just done.

2 Whisk the eggs in a spotlessly clean, grease-free bowl for at least 30 seconds. Add the lemon juice and continue whisking for an additional 30 seconds.

3 Reduce the heat under the pan of bouillon and pasta until the bouillon is not boiling.

4 Gradually add 4–5 tablespoons of the hot (not boiling) bouillon to the lemon and egg mixture, whisking constantly. Gradually add an additional 1 cup of the bouillon, whisking to prevent the eggs curdling.

5 Gradually pour the lemon and egg mixture into the pan, whisking until the soup thickens slightly. Do not let it boil. Season to taste with salt and pepper.

6 Ladle the soup into warmed soup bowls and sprinkle with the chopped Italian parsley. Serve immediately with fresh bread.

veal & exotic mushroom soup

serves four

1 lb/450 g veal, sliced thinly

1 lb/450 g veal bones

5 cups water

1 small onion

6 peppercorns

1 tsp cloves

pinch of mace

1½ cups exotic mushrooms,
   such as oyster and shiitake,
   chopped coarsely

⅔ cup heavy cream

¾ cup dried vermicelli

1 tbsp cornstarch

3 tbsp milk

salt and pepper

1 Put the veal, bones, and water into a large pan. Bring to a boil over a medium heat. Reduce the heat, add the onion, peppercorns, cloves, and mace and simmer for 3 hours, until the bouillon is reduced by one-third.

2 Strain the bouillon into a clean pan and, using a slotted spoon, skim off any fat on the surface. Add the veal meat to the pan.

3 Add the exotic mushrooms and cream to the pan and bring to a boil over a low heat. Simmer for about 12 minutes, stirring occasionally.

4 Bring a large pan of lightly salted water to a boil over a medium heat. Add the pasta and cook for about 10 minutes, or until done. Drain thoroughly and keep warm.

5 Mix the cornstarch and milk together to form a smooth paste and stir into the soup. Season to taste with salt and pepper and add the pasta. Ladle the soup into 4 warmed soup bowls and serve.

beef & noodle soup

serves four

8 oz/225 g lean beef

1 garlic clove, minced

2 scallions, chopped

3 tbsp soy sauce

1 tsp sesame oil

8 oz/225 g egg noodles

3¾ cups beef bouillon

3 baby corn cobs, sliced

½ leek, shredded

4½ oz/125 g broccoli, cut
  into flowerets

pinch of chili powder

VARIATION

Vary the vegetables used or use those to hand. If preferred, use a few drops of chili sauce instead of chili powder, but remember it is very hot!

1 Using a sharp knife, cut the beef into thin strips and put into a large bowl with the garlic, scallions, soy sauce, and sesame oil.

2 Mix the ingredients together in the bowl, turning the beef to coat. Cover and set aside to marinate in the refrigerator for 30 minutes.

3 Bring a pan of water to a boil over a medium heat. Add the noodles and cook for 3–4 minutes. Drain thoroughly and set aside.

4 Put the beef bouillon into a large pan and bring to a boil over a medium heat. Add the beef, with the marinade, the corn, shredded leek, and broccoli. Reduce the heat, cover and simmer for 7–10 minutes, or until the beef and vegetables are tender.

5 Stir in the cooked noodles and chili powder and cook for an additional 2–3 minutes.

6 Ladle the soup into 4 warmed bowls and serve immediately.

italian fish stew

serves four

2 tbsp olive oil

2 red onions, chopped finely

1 garlic clove, minced

2 zucchini, sliced

14 oz/400 g canned
   chopped tomatoes

3¾ cups fish or vegetable bouillon

¾ cup small dried pasta shapes

12 oz/350 g firm white fish, such
   as cod, haddock, or hake

1 tbsp chopped fresh basil or
   oregano or 1 tsp dried oregano

1 tsp finely grated lemon peel

1 tbsp cornstarch

1 tbsp water

salt and pepper

4 fresh basil or oregano sprigs,
   to garnish

1 Heat the oil in a large pan over a low heat. Add the onions and garlic and cook, stirring occasionally, for about 5 minutes, or until softened. Add the zucchini and cook, stirring frequently, for 2–3 minutes.

2 Add the tomatoes and bouillon to the pan and bring to a boil over a medium heat. Add the pasta, bring back to a boil, then reduce the heat, cover and simmer for 5 minutes.

3 Skin and bone the fish, then cut it into chunks. Add to the pan with the basil or oregano and lemon peel and simmer gently for 5 minutes, or until the fish is opaque and flakes easily (take care not to overcook it) and the pasta is done.

4 Blend the cornstarch with the water to form a smooth paste and stir into the stew. Cook for 2 minutes,

stirring constantly, until thickened. Season to taste with salt and pepper.

5 Ladle the stew into 4 large, warmed soup bowls. Garnish with fresh basil or oregano sprigs and serve immediately.

noodle & mushroom soup

serves four

½ oz/15 g dried Chinese
   mushrooms or 4½ oz/125 g
   portobello or crimini mushrooms
4 cups hot vegetable bouillon
4½ oz/125 g thread egg noodles
2 tsp corn oil
3 garlic cloves, minced
1-inch/2.5-cm piece fresh
   gingerroot, shredded finely
½ tsp mushroom catsup
1 tsp light soy sauce
4½ oz/125 g bean sprouts
fresh cilantro leaves, to garnish

1 Soak the Chinese mushrooms (if using) for at least 30 minutes in 1¼ cups of the bouillon. Remove the stalks and discard, then slice the mushrooms. Set aside the bouillon.

2 Bring a large pan of water to a boil over a medium heat. Add the noodles and cook for 2–3 minutes. Drain well and rinse. Set aside.

3 Heat the oil over a high heat in a large skillet. Add the garlic and ginger, stir, and add the mushrooms. Cook, stirring, for 2 minutes.

COOK'S TIP
Rice noodles contain no fat and are ideal for for anyone on a low-fat diet.

4 Add the remaining vegetable bouillon with the reserved bouillon and bring to a boil over a medium heat. Add the mushroom catsup and soy sauce.

5 Stir in the bean sprouts and cook until tender. Put some noodles into each bowl and ladle the soup on top. Garnish with cilantro and serve.

mussel & potato soup

serves four

1 lb 10 oz/750 g mussels

2 tbsp olive oil

7 tbsp unsalted butter

2 slices rindless fatty bacon, chopped

1 onion, chopped

2 garlic cloves, chopped finely

½ cup all-purpose flour

1 lb/450 g potatoes, sliced thinly

¾ cup dried conchigliette

1¼ cups heavy cream

1 tbsp lemon juice

2 egg yolks

salt and pepper

2 tbsp finely chopped fresh parsley,
    to garnish

1 Pull off the "beards" from the mussels and scrub them under cold water for 5 minutes. Discard any mussels that refuse to close when sharply tapped with a knife.

2 Bring a large pan of water to a boil over a medium heat. Add the mussels, oil, and a little pepper and cook until the mussels open.

3 Drain the mussels and set aside the cooking liquid. Discard any mussels that remain closed. Remove the mussels from their shells.

4 Melt the butter in a large pan over a low heat. Add the bacon, onion, and garlic and cook for about 4 minutes. Carefully stir in the flour. Measure 5 cups of the reserved cooking liquid and stir it into the pan.

5 Add the potatoes to the pan and simmer for 5 minutes. Add the pasta, then simmer for 10 minutes.

6 Add the cream and lemon juice, season to taste with salt and pepper, then add the mussels to the pan.

7 Blend the egg yolks with 1–2 tablespoons of the remaining cooking liquid, stir into the pan and cook for 4 minutes.

8 Ladle the soup into 4 large, warmed soup bowls, garnish with the chopped parsley and serve immediately.

Light Meals

Recipes for snacks and light meals offer something for every taste, including vegetables, meat, and fish dishes. These recipes are suitable for when you are not too hungry, but still a bit peckish, or if you are in a hurry and want to eat something quick, but still nutritious and tasty. Try the mouthwatering Italian flavors of Ravioli alla Parmigiana or an Italian-style omelet—they are sure to satisfy even the most discerning tastebuds. All of the recipes in this chapter are quick to prepare and easy to cook, and are sure to become staples in your Italian culinary repertoire.

ravioli alla parmigiana

serves four

285 g/10 oz Homemade Pasta
Dough (see page 24), made
without fresh tarragon

5 cups veal bouillon

1 egg white, beaten

freshly grated Parmesan cheese,
to serve

FILLING

1 cup freshly grated
Parmesan cheese

1⅔ cup fine white bread crumbs

2 eggs

½ cup Espagnole Sauce
(see Cook's Tip)

1 small onion, chopped finely

1 tsp freshly grated nutmeg

1 Make the Homemade Pasta
Dough (see page 24). Carefully
roll out 2 sheets of the pasta dough on
a lightly floured counter and cover with
a damp dish towel while you make the
filling for the ravioli.

2 To make the ravioli filling, mix the
Parmesan cheese, bread crumbs,
eggs, Espagnole Sauce (see Cook's
Tip), onion, and the freshly grated
nutmeg together in a large bowl.

3 Put spoonfuls of the filling at
regular intervals on 1 sheet of the
pasta dough. Cover with the second
sheet of dough, then cut into squares
and seal the edges with egg white.

4 Bring the veal bouillon to a boil in
a large pan over a medium heat.
Add the ravioli and cook for about
15 minutes, or until cooked through.

5 Transfer the ravioli to 4 large,
warmed serving bowls, sprinkle
generously with Parmesan cheese and
serve immediately.

COOK'S TIP

For Espagnole Sauce, melt 2 tbsp
butter and stir in ¼ cup all-
purpose flour. Cook over a low
heat, stirring, until lightly
colored. Add 1 tsp tomato paste,
then stir in scant 2 cups hot veal
bouillon, 1 tbsp Madeira and
1½ tsp white wine vinegar. Dice
1 oz/25 g each bacon, carrot, and
onion and ½ oz/15 g each celery,
leek, and fennel. Cook with a
fresh thyme sprig and a bay leaf
in oil until soft. Drain, add to the
sauce and simmer for 2–3 hours.
Strain before using.

smoked ham linguini

serves four

1 lb/450 g dried linguini

1 lb/450 g broccoli flowerets

⅝ cup Italian Cheese Sauce
   (see page 7)

8 oz/225 g Italian smoked ham

salt and pepper

1 Bring a large pan of lightly salted water to a boil over a medium heat. Add the pasta and broccoli and cook for 10 minutes, or until the pasta is tender, but still firm to the bite.

2 Drain the pasta and broccoli thoroughly, then set aside and keep warm.

3 Meanwhile, make the Italian Cheese Sauce (see page 7).

4 Cut the Italian smoked ham into thin strips. Toss the pasta, broccoli, and ham into the Italian Cheese Sauce, then gently warm through over a low heat.

5 Transfer the pasta mixture to a large, warmed serving dish. Sprinkle with pepper and serve.

creamed veal kidneys with pesto sauce

serves four

5 tbsp butter

12 veal kidneys, trimmed and
    sliced thinly

1½ cups white mushrooms, sliced

1 tsp English mustard

pinch of freshly grated gingerroot

2 tbsp dry sherry

⅝ cup heavy cream

2 tbsp Pesto Sauce (see page 13)

3½ cups dried penne

4 slices of hot toast cut
    into triangles

salt and pepper

4 fresh parsley sprigs, to garnish

1 Melt the butter in a large skillet
over a low heat. Add the kidneys
and cook for 4 minutes. Transfer to an
ovenproof dish and keep warm.

2 Add the mushrooms to the skillet,
and cook for about 2 minutes.

3 Add the mustard and ginger to
the skillet. Season to taste with
salt and pepper. Cook for 2 minutes,
then add the sherry, cream, and Pesto
Sauce (see page 13). Cook for an
additional 3 minutes, then pour the
sauce over the kidneys. Cook in a
preheated oven at 375°F/190°C, for
about 10 minutes.

4 Meanwhile, bring a large pan of
lightly salted water to a boil over
a medium heat. Add the pasta and
cook until done. Drain the pasta
thoroughly and transfer to 4 large,
warmed serving plates.

5 Put the kidneys in the sauce on
top of the pasta. Put a few
triangles of hot toast around the
kidneys, garnish with fresh parsley
sprigs and serve immediately.

chicken scallops

serves four

1½ cups dried short-cut macaroni, or
   other short pasta shapes
2 tbsp vegetable oil, plus extra
   for brushing
1 onion, chopped finely
3 rashers unsmoked Canadian
   bacon, rind removed, chopped
4¼ oz/125 g white mushrooms,
   sliced thinly or chopped
6 oz/175 g cooked chicken, diced
¾ cup unsweetened, plain yogurt
4 tbsp dry bread crumbs
½ cup freshly grated cheddar cheese
salt and pepper
fresh Italian parsley sprigs,
   to garnish

1 Bring a large pan of lightly salted
water to a boil over a medium
heat. Add the pasta and cook for about
8–10 minutes, or until done. Drain the
pasta, return to the pan, and cover.

2 Heat the oil in a large pan over a
medium heat. Add the onion and
cook until translucent. Add the
bacon and mushrooms and cook for
3–4 minutes, stirring once or twice.

3 Stir in the cooked pasta, chicken,
and plain yogurt. Season to taste
with salt and pepper.

4 Brush 4 large scallop shells with a
little oil. Spoon in the chicken
mixture and smooth with a spoon to
make neat mounds.

5 Mix the bread crumbs and cheese
together and sprinkle over the top
of the shells. Press the topping into the
chicken mixture, and cook under a
preheated broiler for 4–5 minutes, or
until golden brown and bubbling.
Garnish with parsley sprigs and serve

chorizo & exotic mushrooms

serves six

1 lb 7 oz/650 g dried vermicelli

½ cup olive oil

2 garlic cloves, chopped finely

4½ oz/125 g chorizo, sliced

8 oz/225 g exotic mushrooms

3 fresh red chiles, chopped

2 tbsp freshly grated
    Parmesan cheese

salt and pepper

10 anchovy fillets, to garnish

COOK'S TIP

Always obtain exotic mushrooms
from a reliable source and never
pick them yourself unless you are
absolutely certain of their
identity. If you can't find exotic
mushrooms, use portobello or
crimini mushrooms or a mixture
of the two instead.

1 Bring a large pan of lightly salted water to a boil over a medium heat. Add the pasta and cook until just done. Drain the pasta thoroughly, put onto a large, warmed serving plate, and keep warm.

2 Meanwhile, heat the oil in a large skillet over a low heat. Add the garlic and cook for 1 minute. Add the chorizo and exotic mushrooms and cook for 4 minutes, then add the red chiles and cook for 1 minute, or until the mushrooms are cooked through.

3 Pour the chorizo and exotic mushroom mixture over the pasta and season to taste with salt and pepper. Transfer to 4 warmed serving plates, sprinkle over the Parmesan cheese and garnish with a lattice of anchovy fillets. Serve immediately.

spaghetti with tomato & anchovy sauce

serves four

3 tbsp olive oil

2 garlic cloves, finely chopped

10 canned anchovy fillets, drained
   and chopped

scant 1 cup black olives, pitted
   and chopped

1 tbsp capers, drained and rinsed

1 lb/450 g plum tomatoes, peeled,
   seeded, and chopped

pinch of cayenne pepper

14 oz/400 g dried spaghetti

2 tbsp chopped fresh parsley,
   to garnish (optional)

VARIATION

You can substitute 14 oz/
400 g canned chopped tomatoes
and their can juices for the fresh
tomatoes, if you prefer.

1 Heat the olive oil in a heavy-
bottom skillet. Add the garlic and
cook over low heat, stirring frequently,
for 2 minutes. Add the anchovies and
mash them to a pulp with a fork. Add
the olives, capers, and tomatoes, and
season to taste with cayenne pepper.
Cover and let simmer for 25 minutes.

2 Meanwhile, bring a large heavy-
bottom pan of lightly salted water
to a boil. Add the pasta, return to a
boil, and cook for 8–10 minutes, or
until tender but still firm to the bite.
Drain well and transfer to a warmed
serving dish.

3 Spoon the anchovy sauce into
the dish and toss the pasta,
using 2 large forks. Garnish with
the chopped parsley, if using, and
serve immediately.

43

spaghetti alla carbonara

serves four

15 oz/425 g dried spaghetti

1 tbsp olive oil

1 large onion, sliced thinly

2 garlic cloves, chopped

6 oz/175 g rindless bacon, cut into
thin strips

2 tbsp butter

1½ cups mushrooms, sliced thinly

1¼ cups heavy cream

3 eggs, beaten

1 cup freshly grated Parmesan
cheese, plus extra to
serve (optional)

salt and pepper

fresh sage sprigs, to garnish

COOK'S TIP

The key to success with this
recipe is not to overcook the
egg. That is why it is important
to keep all the ingredients
hot enough just to cook the
egg—work rapidly to avoid
scrambling it.

1 Bring a large pan of lightly salted water to a boil over a medium heat. Add the pasta and cook for about 8–10 minutes, or until done. Drain the pasta thoroughly, return to the pan, and keep warm.

2 Meanwhile, heat the remaining oil in a skillet over a medium heat. Add the onion and cook until translucent. Add the garlic and bacon and cook until the bacon is crisp. Transfer to a warmed plate.

3 Melt the butter in the skillet over a low heat. Add the mushrooms and cook for 3–4 minutes. Return the bacon mixture to the skillet. Cover and keep warm.

4 Mix the cream, eggs, and cheese together in a large bowl, then season to taste with salt and pepper.

5 Working very quickly, tip the pasta into the bacon and mushroom mixture and pour over the eggs. Using 2 forks, toss the pasta quickly into the egg and cream mixture. Garnish with sage sprigs and serve immediately with extra Parmesan cheese, if you wish.

tricolor timballini

serves four

1 tbsp butter, softened

1 cup dry white bread crumbs

6 oz/175 g dried tricolor spaghetti,
    broken into 2-inch/5-cm lengths

2 tbsp olive oil

1 egg yolk

1 cup freshly grated Swiss cheese

1¼ cups Bechamel Sauce
    (see page 98)

1 onion, chopped finely

1 bay leaf

⅔ cup dry white wine

⅔ cup strained tomatoes

1 tbsp tomato paste

salt and pepper

1 Lightly oil 4 ¾-cup molds or ramekins with the butter. Evenly coat the insides with half the bread crumbs.

2 Bring a pan of lightly salted water to a boil over a medium heat. Add the pasta and cook for about 8–10 minutes, or until done. Drain the pasta thoroughly and transfer to a mixing bowl. Add the egg yolk and cheese to the pasta and season to taste with salt and pepper.

3 Stir the Bechamel Sauce (see page 98) into the pasta and mix well. Spoon the pasta mixture into the prepared molds and sprinkle the remaining bread crumbs over the top.

4 Stand the molds on a cookie sheet and cook in a preheated oven at 425°F/220°C, for 20 minutes. Remove the cookie sheet from the oven and set the molds aside for 10 minutes.

5 To make the sauce, heat the oil in a pan over a low heat. Add the onion and bay leaf and cook for 2–3 minutes. Stir in the wine, strained tomatoes, and tomato paste and season to taste with salt and pepper. Simmer for 20 minutes until thickened. Remove the bay leaf and discard.

6 Turn the timballini out onto 4 large, warmed serving plates and serve immediately with the tomato sauce.

pasta omelet

serves two

4 tbsp olive oil

1 small onion, chopped

1 fennel bulb, sliced thinly

4 oz/115 g potato, diced

1 garlic clove, chopped

4 eggs

1 tbsp chopped fresh Italian parsley

pinch of chili powder

2¼ cups cooked short pasta

2 tbsp stuffed green olives, halved

salt and pepper

fresh marjoram sprigs, to garnish

tomato salad, to serve

1 Heat half the oil in a heavy skillet over a low heat. Add the onion, fennel, and potato and cook, stirring occasionally, for 8–10 minutes, or until the potato is just tender.

2 Stir in the garlic and cook for 1 minute. Remove the skillet from the heat, transfer the vegetables to a plate and set aside.

3 Beat the eggs until frothy. Stir in the parsley and season with salt, pepper, and a pinch of chili powder.

4 Heat 1 tablespoon of the remaining oil in a clean skillet. Add half the egg mixture to the skillet, then add the cooked vegetables, pasta, and half the olives. Pour in the remaining egg mixture and cook until the sides start to set.

5 Lift up the edges of the omelet with a spatula to let the uncooked egg to spread underneath. Cook until the underside is light golden brown.

6 Slide the omelet out of the skillet onto a plate. Wipe the pan with paper towels and heat the remaining oil. Invert the omelet into the pan and cook until the other side is golden.

7 Slide the omelet onto a large, warmed serving dish and garnish with the remaining olives and marjoram sprigs. Cut into wedges and serve with a tomato salad.

spaghetti with ricotta cheese sauce

serves four

12 oz/350 g dried spaghetti

3 tbsp butter

2 tbsp chopped fresh Italian parsley

salt and pepper

fresh Italian parsley sprigs,
    to garnish

SAUCE

1 cup freshly ground almonds

½ cup ricotta cheese

pinch of freshly grated nutmeg

pinch of ground cinnamon

⅔ cup sour cream

2 tbsp olive oil

½ cup hot chicken bouillon

1 tbsp pine nuts

COOK'S TIP

Use 2 large forks to toss spaghetti or other long pasta, so that it is thoroughly coated with the sauce. Special spaghetti forks are available from some cookware departments and large kitchen stores.

1 Bring a pan of lightly salted water to a boil over a medium heat. Add the pasta and cook for about 8–10 minutes, or until done.

2 Drain the pasta thoroughly, then return to the pan and toss the pasta with the butter and chopped parsley. Set the pan aside, cover, and keep warm.

3 To make the sauce, mix the ground almonds, ricotta cheese, nutmeg, cinnamon, and sour cream together in a small pan and stir over low heat to a thick paste. Gradually stir in the oil. When the oil has been fully incorporated, gradually stir in the hot chicken bouillon, until smooth. Season with pepper to taste.

4 Transfer the pasta to a large, warmed serving dish, pour the sauce over it, and toss together well with 2 forks (see Cook's Tip). Sprinkle over the pine nuts, garnish with the sprigs of fresh Italian parsley, and serve immediately.

tagliatelle with garlic butter

serves four

3 cups white bread flour, plus extra
    for dredging

2 tsp salt

4 eggs, beaten

2 tbsp olive oil

5 tbsp butter, melted

3 garlic cloves, chopped finely

2 tbsp chopped fresh parsley

pepper

1 Sift the flour into a large bowl and stir in the salt.

2 Make a well in the center of the dry ingredients and add the eggs and the oil. Using a wooden spoon, stir in the eggs, gradually drawing in the flour. After a few minutes the dough will be too stiff to use a spoon and you will need to use your fingers.

3 Once all of the flour has been incorporated, turn the dough out onto a lightly floured counter and knead for about 5 minutes, or until smooth and elastic. If you find the dough is too wet, add a little more flour and continue kneading. Cover with plastic wrap and chill in the refrigerator for about 30 minutes. This makes the dough easier to roll and less likely to tear.

4 Roll out the pasta dough thinly and create the pasta shapes required. This can be done by hand or using a pasta machine. Results from a machine are usually neater and thinner, but not necessarily better.

5 To make the tagliatelle by hand, fold the thinly rolled pasta sheets into 3 and cut out long, thin strips, about ½-inch/1-cm wide.

6 Bring a large pan of water to a boil over a medium heat. Add the pasta and cook for 2–3 minutes, or until done. The texture should have a slight bite to it. Drain and return the pasta to the pan.

7 Mix the butter, garlic, and parsley together in a small bowl. Stir into the pasta, season with a little pepper to taste, and serve immediately.

tagliarini with gorgonzola

serves four

2 tbsp butter

8 oz/225 g Gorgonzola cheese,
    crumbled coarsely

⅝ cup heavy cream

2 tbsp dry white wine

1 tsp cornstarch

4 fresh sage sprigs, chopped finely

14 oz/400 g dried tagliarini

2 tbsp olive oil

salt and white pepper

1 fresh sage sprig, to garnish

1 Melt the butter in a heavy-bottomed pan over a low heat. Stir in 6 oz/175 g of the Gorgonzola cheese and melt for about 2 minutes.

2 Add the cream, wine, and cornstarch and beat with a wooden spoon until blended.

3 Stir in the sage and season to taste with salt and white pepper. Bring to a boil over a low heat, beating constantly, until the sauce thickens. Remove from the heat and set aside while you cook the pasta.

4 Bring a large pan of lightly salted water to a boil over a medium heat. Add the pasta and cook for 12–14 minutes, or until done. Drain the pasta thoroughly, and toss in the oil. Transfer the pasta to a warmed serving dish and keep warm.

5 Return the pan containing the sauce to a low heat and warm through, beating constantly. Spoon the Gorgonzola sauce over the pasta. Garnish with a fresh sage sprig and sprinkle over the remaining cheese. Serve immediately.

COOK'S TIP

Gorgonzola is one of the world's oldest veined cheeses. When buying, check that it is creamy yellow with green veining. Avoid hard or discolored cheese. It should have a rich, piquant aroma, not a bitter smell.

fettuccine all' alfredo

serves four

2 tbsp butter

scant 1 cup heavy cream

1 lb/450 g fresh fettuccine

1 cup freshly grated Parmesan
   cheese, plus extra to serve

pinch of freshly grated nutmeg

salt and pepper

1 fresh Italian parsley sprig,
   to garnish

VARIATION

This classic Roman dish is often
served with the addition of ham
and peas. Add 2 cups shelled
cooked peas and 6 oz/175 g ham
strips with the cheese in step 4.

---

1 Put the butter and ⅔ cup of the
cream in a large pan and bring
the mixture to a boil over a medium
heat. Reduce the heat, then simmer
gently for about 1½ minutes, or until
the cream has thickened slightly.

2 Meanwhile, bring a large pan of
lightly salted water to a boil over
a medium heat. Add the pasta and
cook for about 2–3 minutes, or until
done Drain the pasta thoroughly and
return to the pan, then pour over the
cream sauce.

3 Toss the pasta in the sauce over a
low heat until thoroughly coated.

4 Add the remaining cream,
Parmesan cheese, and nutmeg to
the pasta mixture, and season to taste
with salt and pepper. Toss the pasta
thoroughly in the mixture while gently
heating through.

5 Transfer the pasta mixture to a
large, warmed serving plate and
garnish with a fresh parsley sprig.
Serve immediately, handing extra
grated Parmesan cheese separately.

rotelle with spicy italian sauce

serves four

⅞ cup Italian Red Wine Sauce
(see page 96)

4 tbsp olive oil

3 garlic cloves, minced

2 fresh red chiles, chopped

1 fresh green chile, chopped

3½ cups dried rotelle

salt and pepper

1 Make the Italian Red Wine Sauce (see page 96).

2 Heat the oil in a pan over a low heat. Add the garlic and chiles and cook for 3 minutes.

3 Stir in the Italian Red Wine Sauce, season to taste with salt and pepper and simmer gently over a low heat for 20 minutes.

4 Bring a large pan of lightly salted water to a boil over a medium heat. Add the pasta and cook for about 8 minutes, or until done. Drain the pasta thoroughly.

5 Toss the pasta in the spicy sauce, then transfer to a warmed serving dish and serve immediately.

spaghetti olio e aglio

serves four

½ cup olive oil

3 garlic cloves, minced

1 lb/450 g fresh spaghetti

3 tbsp coarsely chopped
   fresh parsley

salt and pepper

1 Heat the oil in a medium-size heavy-bottomed pan over a low heat. Add the garlic and a pinch of salt and cook, stirring constantly, until golden brown, then remove the pan from the heat. Do not let the garlic burn as it will taint the flavor of the oil. (If it does burn, you will have to start all over again!)

2 Meanwhile, bring a large pan of lightly salted water to a boil over a medium heat. Add the pasta and cook for about 2–3 minutes, or until

done. Drain the pasta thoroughly and return to the pan.

3 Add the oil and garlic mixture to the pasta and toss to coat thoroughly. Season with pepper to taste, add the chopped fresh parsley and toss to coat again.

4 Transfer the pasta to a large, warmed serving dish and serve.

penne with muscoli fritti nell' olio

serves four–six

3½ cups dried penne

1 lb/450 g mussels, cooked
and shelled

1 tsp sea salt

½ cup olive oil

⅔ cup all-purpose flour

½ cup sun-dried tomatoes, sliced

2 tbsp chopped fresh basil leaves

salt and pepper

TO GARNISH

1 lemon, sliced thinly

fresh basil sprigs

VARIATION

You could substitute clams for
the mussels. If using live clams,
try the smaller varieties, such
as Venus.

1 Bring a large pan of lightly salted water to a boil over a medium heat. Add the pasta and cook for about 8–10 minutes, or until done.

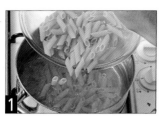

2 Drain the pasta thoroughly and put into a large, warmed serving dish. Set aside and keep warm while you cook the mussels.

3 Lightly sprinkle the mussels with the sea salt. Season the flour with salt and pepper to taste, sprinkle into a bowl, and toss the mussels in the flour until coated.

4 Heat the remaining oil in a large skillet over a medium heat. Add the mussels and cook, stirring frequently, until golden brown.

5 Toss the mussels with the pasta and sprinkle with the sun-dried tomatoes and basil. Transfer to 4 plates, garnish with lemon slices and fresh basil sprigs. Serve immediately.

COOK'S TIP

Sun-dried tomatoes have been
used in Mediterranean countries
for a long time, but have become
popular elsewhere only quite
recently. They are dried and often
preserved in oil. They have a
concentrated, almost roasted
flavor and a dense texture. They
should be drained and chopped
or sliced before using.

spicy tomato tagliatelle

serves four

3 tbsp butter

1 onion, chopped finely

1 garlic clove, minced

2 small fresh red chiles, seeded
  and diced

1 lb/450 g tomatoes, peeled,
  seeded, and diced

¾ cup vegetable bouillon

2 tbsp tomato paste

1 tsp sugar

1 lb 7 oz/650 g fresh green
  and white tagliatelle or
  12 oz/350 g dried tagliatelle

salt and pepper

1 Melt the butter in a large pan over a medium-low heat. Add the onion and garlic and cook for about 3–4 minutes, or until softened.

2 Add the chiles to the pan and continue cooking for about 2 minutes.

3 Add the tomatoes and bouillon, then reduce the heat and simmer for 10 minutes, stirring.

4 Pour the sauce into a food processor and blend for 1 minute, or until smooth. Alternatively, push the sauce through a strainer.

5 Return the sauce to the pan and add the tomato paste, sugar, and salt and pepper to taste. Gently heat over a low heat, until piping hot.

6 Bring a large pan of lightly salted water to a boil over a medium heat. Add the pasta and cook until done. Drain the pasta thoroughly. Transfer to 4 warmed serving plates and serve tossed in the tomato sauce.

pasta with cheese & broccoli

serves four

10½ oz/300 g dried tagliatelle
   tricolore (plain, spinach- and
   tomato-flavored noodles)
2½ cups broccoli, broken into
   small flowerets
1½ cups mascarpone cheese
1 cup blue cheese, chopped
1 tbsp chopped fresh oregano
2 tbsp butter
salt and pepper
4 fresh oregano sprigs, to garnish
freshly grated Parmesan cheese,
   to serve

1 Bring a large pan of lightly salted water to a boil over a medium heat. Add the pasta and cook for 8–10 minutes, or until done.

2 Bring a pan of salted water to a boil over a medium heat. Add the broccoli and cook. Avoid overcooking, so it retains its color and texture.

3 Heat the mascarpone and blue cheeses together in a large pan over a low heat until melted. Stir in the chopped oregano and season to taste. with salt and pepper.

4 Drain the pasta thoroughly and return to the pan. Add the butter and toss the pasta until coated thoroughly. Drain the broccoli well and add to the pasta with the sauce, tossing gently to mix.

5 Transfer the pasta to 4 large, warmed serving plates and garnish with fresh oregano sprigs. Serve with Parmesan cheese.

penne & butternut squash

serves four

2 tbsp olive oil

1 garlic clove, minced

1 cup fresh white bread crumbs

1 lb 2 oz/500 g butternut squash,
    peeled and seeded

8 tbsp water

1 lb 2 oz/500 g fresh penne, or
    other pasta shapes

1 tbsp butter

1 onion, sliced

4 oz/115 g ham, cut into strips

scant 1 cup light cream

½ cup freshly grated cheddar cheese

2 tbsp chopped fresh parsley

salt and pepper

COOK'S TIP

If the squash weighs more than
is needed for this recipe, blanch
the excess for 3–4 minutes on
HIGH in a covered bowl with a
little water. Drain, cool, and put
into a freezer bag. Store in the
freezer for up to 3 months.

1 Mix the oil, garlic, and bread
crumbs together and spread out
on a large plate. Cook in the
microwave on HIGH for 4–5 minutes,
stirring every minute, until crisp and
starting to brown. Remove from the
microwave and set aside.

2 Dice the squash and put into a
large bowl with half the water.
Cover and cook on HIGH for about
8–9 minutes, stirring occasionally. Let
stand for 2 minutes.

3 Put the pasta into a large bowl,
add a little salt, and pour over
boiling water to cover by 1 inch/
2.5 cm. Cover and cook on HIGH for
5 minutes, stirring once, until the
pasta is done. Let stand, covered, for
1 minute before draining.

4 Put the butter and onion into a
large bowl. Cover and cook on
HIGH for 3 minutes.

5 Using a fork, coarsely mash the
squash. Add to the onion with
the pasta, ham, cream, cheese, parsley,
and the remaining water. Season
generously with salt and pepper and
mix well. Cover and cook on HIGH for
4 minutes until heated through.

6 Transfer the pasta to 4 warmed
serving plates and sprinkle with
the crisp garlic crumbs. Serve.

pasta with basil & pine nut pesto

serves four

about 40 fresh basil leaves

3 garlic cloves, minced

¼ cup pine nuts

½ cup finely grated
   Parmesan cheese

2–3 tbsp extra virgin olive oil

salt and pepper

1 lb 7 oz/650 g fresh pasta or
   12 oz/350 g dried pasta

1 Rinse the basil leaves and pat them dry on paper towels.

2 Put the basil leaves, garlic, pine nuts, and grated Parmesan cheese into a food processor and blend for about 30 seconds, or until smooth. Alternatively, put the ingredients into a mortar and pound with a pestle.

3 If you are using a food processor, keep the motor running and slowly add the oil. Alternatively, add the oil drop by drop while stirring. Season to taste with salt and pepper.

4 Meanwhile, bring a large pan of lightly salted water to a boil over a medium heat. Add the pasta and cook until done. Drain the pasta thoroughly.

5 Transfer the pasta to a serving plate and serve with the pesto. Toss to mix well and serve hot.

fettuccine with walnut sauce

serves four–six

2 thick slices whole-wheat bread,
   crusts removed

1¼ cups milk

2½ cups shelled walnuts

2 garlic cloves, minced

1 cup pitted ripe black olives

⅔ cup freshly grated
   Parmesan cheese

8 tbsp extra virgin olive oil

⅝ cup heavy cream

1 lb/450 g fresh fettuccine

2–3 tbsp chopped fresh parsley

salt and pepper

1 Put the slices of bread into a large shallow dish, pour over the milk and set aside to soak until all the liquid has been absorbed.

2 Spread the walnuts out onto a cookie sheet and toast in a preheated oven at 375°F/190°C, for about 5 minutes, or until golden. Let cool and set aside until required.

3 Put the soaked bread, walnuts, garlic, olives, Parmesan cheese, and 6 tablespoons of the oil into a food processor and work to make a paste. Season to taste with salt and pepper and stir in the cream.

4 Bring a large pan of lightly salted water to a boil over a medium heat. Add the pasta and cook for about 2–3 minutes, or until done. Drain the pasta thoroughly and toss with the oil.

5 Transfer the pasta to large, warmed serving plates and spoon the olive, garlic, and walnut sauce on top. Sprinkle over the chopped parsley and serve immediately.

spaghetti with smoked salmon

serves four

1 lb/450 g dried spaghetti

1 tbsp olive oil

1 cup heavy cream

⅔ cup whiskey or brandy

4½ oz/125 g smoked salmon

pinch of cayenne pepper

2 tbsp chopped fresh cilantro
    or parsley

¾ cup crumbled feta cheese
    (drained weight)

pepper

fresh cilantro or parsley sprigs,
    to garnish

COOK'S TIP

Serve this rich and luxurious dish
with a salad greens tossed in a
lemony dressing.

1 Bring a large pan of lightly salted water to a boil over a medium heat. Add the pasta and cook until done. Drain the pasta thoroughly, return to the pan and sprinkle over the oil. Cover, shake the pan, set aside, and keep warm.

2 Pour the cream into a small pan and bring to simmering point, but do not let it boil. Pour the whiskey or brandy into another small pan and bring to simmering point, but do not let it boil. Remove both pans from the heat and mix the cream and whiskey or brandy together.

3 Cut the smoked salmon into thin strips and add to the cream mixture. Season to taste with cayenne and pepper. Just before serving, stir in the chopped fresh cilantro or parsley.

4 Transfer the pasta to a warmed serving dish, pour over the sauce and toss thoroughly with 2 large forks. Transfer to 4 warmed plates, sprinkle over the feta cheese and garnish with the cilantro sprigs. Serve immediately.

pasta & sicilian sauce

serves four

1 lb/450 g tomatoes, halved

¼ cup pine nuts

⅓ cup golden raisins

1¾ oz/50 g canned anchovy fillets,
    drained and halved lengthwise

2 tbsp concentrated tomato paste

1lb 8 oz/675 g fresh penne or
    12 oz/350 g dried penne

COOK'S TIP

If you are making fresh pasta,
remember that pasta dough
prefers warm conditions and
responds well to handling. Do
not let chill and do not use a
marble counter for kneading.

1 Put the tomatoes under a
preheated hot broiler and cook for
about 10 minutes. Let cool. Once cool
enough to handle, peel off the skin
and dice the flesh.

2 Put the pine nuts onto a cookie
sheet and lightly toast under the
broiler for 2–3 minutes until golden.

3 Put the golden raisins into a bowl
and pour over enough warm
water to cover. Let soak for 20 minutes,
then drain thoroughly.

4 Put the tomatoes, pine nuts, and
golden raisins into a small pan
and warm over a low heat.

5 Add the anchovies and tomato
paste to the pan and cook for an
additional 2–3 minutes, or until hot.

6 Bring a large pan of lightly salted
water to a boil over a medium
heat. Add the pasta and cook until
done. Drain the pasta thoroughly.

7 Transfer the pasta to 4 large,
warmed serving plates and serve
with the hot Sicilian sauce.

baked rigatoni filled with tuna & ricotta

serves four

1 tbsp butter for greasing

1 lb/450 g dried rigatoni

1 tbsp olive oil

7 oz/200 g canned flaked
  tuna, drained

1 cup ricotta cheese

½ cup heavy cream

2 cups freshly grated
  Parmesan cheese

4 oz/125 g sun-dried tomatoes in
  oil, drained and sliced

salt and pepper

1 Lightly grease a large ovenproof dish with the butter.

2 Bring a large pan of lightly salted water to a boil over a medium heat. Add the pasta tubes and oil, and cook for 8–10 minutes, or until done. Drain the pasta tubes thoroughly and set aside until the pasta tubes are cool enough to handle.

3 Meanwhile, mix the tuna and ricotta cheese together in a bowl to form a soft paste. Spoon the mixture into a pastry bag and use to fill the pasta tubes. Arrange the filled pasta tubes side by side in a single layer in the prepared ovenproof dish.

4 To make the sauce, mix the cream and Parmesan cheese together and season to taste with salt and pepper. Spoon the sauce over the filled pasta tubes in the dish and top with the sun-dried tomatoes, arranged in a criss-cross pattern.

5 Cook in a preheated oven at 400°F/200°C, for 20 minutes, or until piping hot. Serve immediately straight from the dish.

fettuccine with anchovy & spinach sauce

serves four

2 lb/900 g fresh, young
   spinach leaves

14 oz/400 g dried fettuccine

5 tbsp olive oil

3 tbsp pine nuts

3 garlic cloves, minced

8 canned anchovy fillets, drained
   and chopped

salt

COOK'S TIP

If you are in a hurry, you can use frozen spinach. Thaw and drain it thoroughly, pressing out as much moisture as possible. Cut the leaves into strips and add to the dish with the anchovies in step 4.

1 Trim off any tough spinach stalks. Rinse the spinach leaves and put them into a large pan with the water that is clinging to them after washing. Cover and cook over a high heat, shaking the pan from time to time, until the spinach has wilted, but retains its color. Drain thoroughly, then set aside and keep warm.

2 Bring a large pan of lightly salted water to a boil over a medium heat. Add the pasta and cook for about 8–10 minutes, or until done.

3 Meanwhile, heat 4 tablespoons of the oil in a pan. Add the pine nuts and cook until they just turn golden. Remove the pine nuts from the pan and set aside until required.

4 Add the garlic to the pan and cook until golden. Add the anchovies and stir in the wilted spinach. Cook, stirring, for about 2–3 minutes, or until heated through. Return the pine nuts to the pan.

5 Drain the pasta, toss in the remaining oil and transfer to a large, warmed serving dish. Spoon the anchovy and spinach sauce over the pasta and toss lightly. Transfer to 4 warmed serving plates and serve.

pipe rigate with gorgonzola sauce

serves four

14 oz/400 g dried pipe rigate

2 tbsp unsalted butter

6 fresh sage leaves

7 oz/200 g Gorgonzola cheese,
   diced

¾–1 cup heavy cream or
   panna da cucina

2 tbsp dry vermouth

salt and pepper

1 Bring a large heavy-bottom pan of lightly salted water to a boil. Add the pasta, return to a boil, and cook for 8–10 minutes, until tender but still firm to the bite.

2 Meanwhile, melt the butter in a separate heavy-bottom pan. Add the sage leaves and cook, stirring gently, for 1 minute. Remove and set aside the sage leaves. Add the cheese and cook, stirring constantly, over low heat until it has melted. Gradually, stir in ¾ cup of the cream and the vermouth. Season to taste with salt and pepper and cook, stirring, until thickened. Add more cream if the sauce seems too thick.

3 Drain the pasta well and transfer to a warmed serving dish. Add the Gorgonzola sauce, toss well to mix, and serve immediately, garnished with the reserved sage leaves.

COOK'S TIP

Gorgonzola should be creamy colored with pale-green marbling, and have a pleasant aroma. Do not buy it if it is hard, discolored, or smelly.

pasta & herring salad

serves four

2¼ cups dried pasta shells

4 tbsp olive oil

14 oz/400 g rollmop herrings
in brine, drained

6 boiled potatoes

2 large tart apples

2 baby frisee lettuces

2 baby beet

4 hard-cooked eggs

6 pickled onions

6 dill pickles

2 tbsp capers

3 tbsp of tarragon vinegar

salt and pepper

1 Bring a large pan of lightly salted water to a boil over a medium heat. Add the pasta and cook for about 8–10 minutes, or until done. Drain the pasta thoroughly, then refresh in cold water.

2 Using a sharp knife, cut the herrings, potatoes, apples, frisee, and beet into small pieces, then put into a large salad bowl.

3 Drain the pasta thoroughly again and add to the salad bowl. Toss lightly with a spoon to mix the pasta and herring mixture together.

4 Carefully shell and slice the eggs and garnish the salad with the egg slices, pickled onions, dill pickles, and capers. Sprinkle with the oil and the tarragon vinegar, then serve the salad immediately.

COOK'S TIP
Store this salad, without the dressing, in a container in the refrigerator.

71

spaghetti with anchovy & pesto sauce

serves four

6 tbsp olive oil

2 garlic cloves, chopped finely

2 oz/55 g canned anchovy
  fillets, drained

1 lb/450 g dried spaghetti

2 oz/55 g pesto sauce
  (store bought)

2 tbsp finely chopped fresh oregano

1 cup freshly grated Parmesan
  cheese, plus extra for
  serving (optional)

salt and pepper

4 fresh oregano sprigs, to garnish

COOK'S TIP

If you find canned anchovies
much too salty, soak them in a
saucer of cold milk for 5 minutes,
drain and pat dry on paper
towels before using.

VARIATION

For a vegetarian alternative of
this recipe, simply substitute
drained sun-dried tomatoes for
the anchovy fillets.

---

1 Heat the oil in a small pan over a medium heat. Add the garlic and cook for 3 minutes.

2 Reduce the heat, stir in the anchovies and cook, stirring occasionally, until the anchovies have completely disintegrated.

3 Bring a large pan of lightly salted water to a boil over a medium heat. Add the pasta and cook for about 8–10 minutes, or until done.

4 Add the pesto sauce and the chopped oregano to the anchovy mixture, then season with pepper to taste.

5 Using a slotted spoon, drain the pasta and transfer to 4 large, warmed serving dishes. Pour the pesto sauce over the pasta, then sprinkle over the Parmesan cheese.

6 Garnish with oregano sprigs and serve with extra cheese (if using).

pasta salad with red & white cabbage

serves four

2¼ cups dried short-cut macaroni

1 large red cabbage, shredded

1 large white cabbage, shredded

2 large apples, diced

9 oz/250 g cooked smoked bacon
   or ham, diced

4 tbsp olive oil

8 tbsp wine vinegar

1 tbsp sugar

salt and pepper

VARIATION

An alternative dressing for this
salad can be made with 4 tbsp of
olive oil, 4 tbsp of red wine,
4 tbsp of red wine vinegar, and
1 tbsp of sugar.

1 Bring a large pan of lightly salted water to a boil over a medium heat. Add the macaroni and cook until done. Drain the macaroni thoroughly, then refresh in cold water. Drain the macaroni again and set aside.

2 Bring a large pan of lightly salted water to a boil over a medium heat. Add the shredded red cabbage and cook for 5 minutes. Drain thoroughly and let cool.

3 Bring a large pan of lightly salted water to a boil over a medium heat. Add the white cabbage and cook for 5 minutes. Drain thoroughly and let cool.

4 Mix the pasta, red cabbage, and apple together in a bowl. Mix the white cabbage and bacon or ham together in a separate bowl.

5 Mix the oil, vinegar, and sugar together in a bowl, then season to taste with salt and pepper. Pour the dressing over each of the 2 cabbage mixtures and, mix them all together. Serve immediately.

pasta & chicken medley

serves two

generous 1–1⅓ cups dried pasta
   shapes, such as twists or bows

2 tbsp mayonnaise

2 tsp bottled pesto sauce

1 tbsp sour cream

6 oz/175g cooked, skinless,
   boneless chicken meat

1–2 celery stalks

4½ oz/125 g black grapes
   (preferably seedless)

1 large carrot

salt and pepper

celery leaves, to garnish

FRENCH DRESSING

1 tsp wine vinegar

1 tbsp extra virgin olive oil

salt and pepper

1 To make the French dressing, whisk all the ingredients together in a small bowl until smooth.

2 Bring a large pan of lightly salted water to a boil over a medium heat. Add the pasta and cook for 8–10 minutes, or until done. Drain the pasta thoroughly, refresh in cold water, and drain again. Transfer to a bowl and mix in the French dressing while still hot, then set aside until cold.

3 Mix the mayonnaise, pesto sauce, and sour cream in a bowl and season to taste with salt and pepper.

4 Cut the chicken into thin strips. Cut the celery diagonally into thin slices. Set aside a few grapes for garnish, halve the rest, and remove any seeds. Cut the carrot into narrow julienne strips.

5 Add the chicken, celery, halved grapes, carrot, and mayonnaise mixture to the cooled pasta. Toss thoroughly to coat the pasta. Taste and adjust the seasoning, if necessary.

6 Arrange the pasta on 2 serving plates and garnish with the black grapes and celery leaves. Serve.

nicoise salad with pasta shells

serves four

3 cups dried small pasta shells

4 oz/115 g green beans

1¾ oz/50 g canned anchovy
  fillets, drained

⅛ cup milk

2 small crisp lettuces

1 lb/450 g or 3 large tomatoes

4 hard-cooked eggs

8 oz/225 g canned tuna, drained

1 cup pitted ripe black olives

salt

VINAIGRETTE DRESSING

¼ cup extra virgin olive oil

2 tbsp white wine vinegar

1 tsp whole-grain mustard

salt and pepper

COOK'S TIP

It is convenient to make salad
dressings in a screw-top jar. Put
all the ingredients in the jar, then
cover securely and shake well to
mix and emulsify the oil.

---

1 Bring a large pan of lightly salted water to a boil over a medium heat. Add the pasta and cook until done. Drain the pasta thoroughly and refresh in cold water.

2 Bring a small pan of lightly salted water to a boil over a medium heat. Add the beans and cook for 10–12 minutes, or until done. Drain thoroughly and refresh in cold water, then drain again and set aside.

3 Put the anchovies into a shallow bowl, then pour over the milk and set aside for 10 minutes. Meanwhile, tear the lettuces into large pieces. Blanch the tomatoes in boiling water for 1–2 minutes, then drain. Skin and coarsely chop the flesh. Shell the eggs and cut into fourths. Cut the tuna into large chunks.

4 Drain the anchovies and the pasta. Put the salad ingredients, the green beans, and the olives into a large bowl and gently mix together.

5 To make the vinaigrette dressing, beat all the dressing ingredients together and keep in the refrigerator until required. Just before serving, pour the vinaigrette dressing over the salad.

rare beef pasta salad

serves four

1 lb/450 g rump or sirloin steak in
1 piece
1⅓ cups dried fusilli
4 tbsp olive oil
2 tbsp lime juice
2 tbsp Thai fish sauce
(see Cook's Tip)
2 tsp honey
4 scallions, sliced
1 cucumber, peeled and cut into
1-inch/2.5-cm chunks
3 tomatoes, cut into wedges
3 tsp finely chopped fresh mint
salt and pepper

COOK'S TIP

Thai fish sauce, also known
as nam pla, is made from salted
anchovies. It has a strong flavor,
so should be used with care.

1 Season the steak with salt and pepper. Broil or pan-fry the steak for about 4 minutes on each side. Let stand for 5 minutes, then slice thinly across the grain.

2 Meanwhile, bring a large pan of lightly salted water to a boil over a medium heat. Add the pasta and cook until done. Drain the pasta thoroughly, then refresh in cold water and drain again. Return the pasta to the pan and toss in the oil.

3 Mix the lime juice, fish sauce, and honey together in a small pan and cook over a medium heat for about 2 minutes.

4 Add the scallions, cucumber, tomatoes, and chopped mint to the pan, then add the steak and mix well. Season with salt to taste.

5 Transfer the pasta to a large, warmed serving dish and top with the steak mixture. Serve just warm or let cool completely.

spicy sausage salad

serves four

1 cup small dried pasta shapes,
  such as elbow tubetti
2 tbsp olive oil
1 medium onion, chopped
2 garlic cloves, minced
1 small yellow bell pepper, seeded
  and cut into very thin sticks
6 oz/175 g spicy pork sausage, such
  as chorizo, Italian pepperoni or
  salami, skinned and sliced
2 tbsp red wine
1 tbsp red wine vinegar
mixed salad greens, chilled
salt

2 Heat the oil in a pan over a medium heat. Add the onion and cook until translucent, stir in the garlic, yellow bell pepper, and sliced sausage, and cook for 3–4 minutes, stirring once or twice.

3 Add the wine, wine vinegar, and reserved pasta to the pan, stir to blend well, and bring the mixture just to a boil over a medium heat.

4 Arrange the chilled salad greens onto 4 serving plates, spoon on the warm sausage and pasta mixture, and serve immediately.

VARIATION

Other suitable sausages include the Italian pepperoni, flavored with chile peppers, fennel, and spices, and one of the many varieties of salami, usually flavored with garlic and pepper.

1 Bring a large pan of lightly salted water to a boil over a medium heat. Add the pasta and cook until done. Drain and set aside.

goat cheese, pear & walnut salad

serves four

2¼ cups dried penne

1 head radicchio, torn into pieces

1 Webbs lettuce, torn into pieces

7 tbsp chopped walnuts

2 ripe pears, cored and diced

⅛ cup arugula, trimmed

2 tbsp lemon juice

5 tbsp olive oil

1 garlic clove, chopped

3 tbsp white wine vinegar

4 tomatoes, cut into fourths

1 small onion, sliced

1 large carrot, grated

9 oz/250 g goat cheese, diced

salt and pepper

COOK'S TIP

Most goat cheese comes from France and there are many varieties, such as Crottin de Chavignol, Chabi, which is very pungent, and Sainte-Maure, which is available in creamery and farmhouse varieties.

1 Bring a large pan of lightly salted water to a boil over a medium heat. Add the pasta and cook until done. Drain the pasta thoroughly and refresh in cold water, then drain again and set aside to cool.

2 Put the radicchio and Webbs lettuce into a large salad bowl and mix together well. Top with the cooled pasta, chopped walnuts, pears, and arugula.

3 Mix the lemon juice, oil, garlic, and vinegar together in a measuring pitcher. Pour the mixture over the salad ingredients and toss to coat the salad leaves well.

4 Add the tomato fourths, onion slices, grated carrot, and diced goat cheese and toss together with 2 forks, until well mixed. Let the salad chill in the refrigerator for about 1 hour before serving.

pasta with pesto vinaigrette

serves six

2 cups dried pasta spirals

4 tomatoes, peeled

½ cup ripe black olives

2 tbsp sun-dried tomatoes in
    oil, drained

2 tbsp pine nuts, toasted

2 tbsp freshly grated Parmesan cheese

1 fresh basil sprig, to garnish

PESTO VINAIGRETTE

4 tbsp chopped fresh basil

1 garlic clove, minced

2 tbsp freshly grated
    Parmesan cheese

4 tbsp olive oil

2 tbsp lemon juice

salt and pepper

1 Bring a large pan of lightly salted water to a boil over a medium heat. Add the pasta and cook for 8–10 minutes, or until done. Drain the pasta thoroughly, rinse well in hot water, then drain again. Set aside.

2 To make the pesto vinaigrette, whisk the basil, garlic, Parmesan cheese, oil, and lemon juice together in a small bowl until well blended. Season with pepper to taste.

3 Put the pasta into a bowl, pour the pesto vinaigrette over it, and toss thoroughly.

4 Cut the tomatoes into wedges. Halve and pit the olives and slice the sun-dried tomatoes. Add the tomatoes, olives, and sun-dried tomatoes to the pasta and toss well.

5 Transfer the pasta to a salad bowl and sprinkle the pine nuts and Parmesan cheese over the top. Garnish with a basil sprig and serve warm.

dolcelatte, nut & pasta salad

serves four

2 cups dried pasta shells

1 cup shelled and halved walnuts

mixed salad greens, such as
    radicchio, escarole, arugula,
    corn salad, and frisee

8 oz/225 g dolcelatte cheese,
    crumbled

salt and pepper

DRESSING

2 tbsp walnut oil

4 tbsp extra virgin olive oil

2 tbsp red wine vinegar

3 To make the dressing, whisk the walnut oil, olive oil, and vinegar together in a small bowl, and season to taste with salt and pepper.

4 Arrange the mixed salad greens in a large serving bowl. Pile the cooled pasta in the center of the salad greens and sprinkle over the dolcelatte cheese. Pour the dressing over the pasta salad, then sprinkle over the walnut halves and toss together to mix well. Serve immediately.

1 Bring a large pan of lightly salted water to a boil over a medium heat. Add the pasta shells and cook until done. Drain the pasta thoroughly and refresh in cold water, then drain again and set aside.

2 Spread out the shelled walnut halves onto a cookie sheet and toast under a preheated hot broiler for 2–3 minutes. Remove and let cool while you make the salad dressing.

avocado, tomato & mozzarella salad

serves four

2 tbsp pine nuts

1½ cups dried fusilli

6 tomatoes

8 oz/225 g mozzarella cheese

1 large avocado pear

2 tbsp lemon juice

3 tbsp chopped fresh basil

salt and pepper

fresh basil sprigs, to garnish

DRESSING

6 tbsp extra virgin olive oil

2 tbsp white wine vinegar

1 tsp whole-grain mustard

pinch of sugar

1 Spread the pine nuts out onto a cookie sheet and toast under a preheated hot broiler for 1–2 minutes. Remove and let cool.

2 Bring a large pan of lightly salted water to a boil over a medium heat. Add the pasta and cook until done. Drain the pasta thoroughly and refresh in cold water. Drain again and let cool.

3 Thinly slice the tomatoes and the mozzarella cheese.

4 Using a sharp knife, cut the avocado pear in half, then remove the pit and skin. Cut into thin slices lengthwise and sprinkle with lemon juice to prevent discoloration.

5 To make the dressing, whisk the oil, vinegar, mustard, and sugar together in a small bowl. Season to taste with salt and pepper.

6 Arrange the tomatoes, mozzarella cheese, and avocado pear alternately in overlapping slices on a large serving plate.

7 Toss the pasta with half the dressing and the chopped basil and season to taste with salt and pepper. Spoon the pasta into the center of the plate and pour over the remaining dressing. Sprinkle over the pine nuts and garnish with fresh basil sprigs. Serve immediately.

marinated eggplant on a bed of linguine

serves four

²⁄₃ cup vegetable bouillon

²⁄₃ cup white wine vinegar

2 tsp balsamic vinegar

3 tbsp olive oil

1 fresh oregano sprig

1 lb/450 g eggplants, peeled and
    sliced thinly

14 oz/400 g dried linguine

MARINADE

2 tbsp extra virgin olive oil

2 garlic cloves, minced

2 tbsp chopped fresh oregano

2 tbsp finely chopped
    roasted almonds

2 tbsp diced red bell pepper

2 tbsp lime juice

grated peel and juice of 1 orange

salt and pepper

1 Put the vegetable bouillon, wine vinegar, and balsamic vinegar into a pan and bring to a boil over a low heat. Add 2 teaspoons of the oil and the oregano sprig and simmer gently for about 1 minute.

2 Add the eggplant slices to the pan, remove from the heat, and set aside for 10 minutes.

3 To make the marinade, mix the oil, garlic, fresh oregano, almonds, red bell pepper, lime juice, orange peel and juice together in a large bowl. Season to taste with salt and pepper.

4 Carefully remove the eggplant slices from the pan with a slotted spoon, and drain well. Add the eggplant slices to the marinade, mixing well to coat. Cover with plastic wrap and chill in the refrigerator for about 12 hours.

5 Bring a large pan of lightly salted water to a boil over a medium heat. Add the pasta and cook for about 8–10 minutes, or until done.

6 Drain the pasta thoroughly and toss with the remaining oil while it is still warm. Arrange the pasta on a serving plate with the eggplant slices and the marinade. Serve immediately.

pasta provencale

serves four

2 cups dried penne

1 tbsp olive oil

2 tbsp pitted ripe black olives,
  drained and chopped

2 tbsp dry-pack sun-dried tomatoes,
  soaked, drained, and chopped

14 oz/400 g canned artichoke
  hearts, drained and halved

4 oz/115 g baby zucchini, trimmed
  and sliced

4 oz/115 g baby plum
  tomatoes, halved

3½ oz/100 g assorted baby
  salad greens

salt and pepper

shredded basil leaves, to garnish

DRESSING

4 tbsp strained tomatoes

2 tbsp low-fat unsweetened yogurt

1 tbsp unsweetened orange juice

1 small bunch fresh basil, shredded

1 Bring a large pan of lightly salted water to a boil over a medium heat. Add the pasta and cook until done. Drain the pasta thoroughly and return to the pan. Stir in the oil, salt and pepper, olives, and sun-dried tomatoes, then let cool.

2 Gently mix the artichokes, zucchini, and plum tomatoes into the cooked pasta. Arrange the salad leaves in a serving bowl.

VARIATION

For a non-vegetarian version, stir 8 oz/225 g canned tuna in brine, drained, and flaked, into the pasta together with the vegetables. Other pasta shapes can be included— look out for farfalle (bows) and rotelle (spoked wheels).

3 To make the dressing, mix all the ingredients together and toss into the vegetables and pasta.

4 Spoon the mixture on top of the salad and garnish with basil.

Meat & Poultry

Pasta and meat or poultry is a classic combination. Dishes range from easy, economic mid-week suppers to sophisticated and elegant meals for special occasions. The recipes in this chapter include many family favorites, such as Spaghetti Bolognese, Tagliatelle with Meatballs, Lasagna Verde, and Cannelloni. There are also some exciting variations on traditional themes, such as Sicilian Spaghetti, Chicken Tortellini, and Chicken & Ham Lasagna. Finally, there is a superb collection of mouthwatering original recipes. Why not try Tagliatelle with Pumpkin & Prosciutto, Pasta & Pork in Cream Sauce, Chicken & lobster on Penne or Breast of Pheasant Lasagna.

pasticcio

serves four

2 cups dried fusilli

4 tbsp heavy cream

1 tbsp olive oil for brushing

salt

fresh rosemary sprigs, to garnish

mixed salad greens, to serve

SAUCE

2 tbsp olive oil

1 onion, sliced thinly

1 red bell pepper, seeded
   and chopped

2 garlic cloves, chopped

5¼ cups ground beef

14 oz/400 g canned
   chopped tomatoes

½ cup dry white wine

2 tbsp chopped fresh parsley

2 oz/55 g canned anchovy fillets,
   drained and chopped

salt and pepper

TOPPING

1¼ cups unsweetened plain yogurt

3 eggs

pinch of freshly grated nutmeg

½ cup freshly grated
   Parmesan cheese

1 Heat the oil in a skillet over a medium heat. Add the onion and red pepper and cook for 3 minutes. Add the garlic and cook for 1 minute. Add the beef and cook until browned.

2 Add the tomatoes and wine and bring to a boil over a medium heat. Reduce the heat and simmer for 20 minutes, or until thickened. Stir in the parsley and anchovies, and season to taste with salt and pepper.

3 Bring a large pan of lightly salted water to a boil over a medium heat. Add the pasta and cook until almost done. Drain and transfer to a bowl. Stir in the cream.

4 For the topping, beat the yogurt, eggs, and nutmeg together.

5 Brush an ovenproof dish with oil. Spoon in half the pasta and cover with half the meat sauce. Repeat, then spread over the topping and sprinkle with the grated Parmesan cheese.

6 Bake in a preheated oven at 375°F/190°C, for 25 minutes, or until golden. Garnish with a rosemary sprig and serve with salad greens.

lasagna verde

serves four

1 tbsp butter for greasing

14 sheets precooked lasagna

generous 3 cups Bechamel Sauce
  (see page 98)

1⅓ cups freshly grated
  mozzarella cheese

1 fresh basil sprig, to garnish

MEAT SAUCE

2 tbsp olive oil

2 cups ground beef

1 large onion, chopped

1 celery stalk, diced

4 garlic cloves, minced

¼ cup all-purpose flour

½ pint beef bouillon

¼ pint red wine

1 tbsp chopped fresh parsley

1 tsp chopped fresh marjoram

1 tsp chopped fresh basil

2 tbsp tomato paste

salt and pepper

1 To make the meat sauce, heat the oil in a large skillet over a medium heat. Add the ground beef and cook, stirring frequently, until browned. Add the onion, celery, and garlic and cook for 3 minutes.

2 Sprinkle over the flour and cook, stirring, for 1 minute. Gradually stir in the bouillon and wine. Season with salt and pepper and add the herbs. Bring to a boil, reduce the heat and simmer for 35 minutes. Add the tomato paste and cook for 10 minutes.

3 Lightly grease an ovenproof dish with the butter. Arrange sheets of lasagna over the bottom of the dish, spoon over a layer of meat sauce, then Bechamel Sauce (see page 98). Repeat the process twice, finishing with a layer of Bechamel Sauce. Sprinkle over the mozzarella cheese.

4 Cook the lasagna in a preheated oven at 375°F/190°C, for 35 minutes, or until the top is golden brown and bubbling. Garnish with a basil sprig and serve immediately straight from the dish.

eggplant cake

serves four

1 eggplant, sliced thinly

4 tbsp olive oil

2 cups dried fusilli

2½ cups Bechamel Sauce
   (see page 98)

¾ cup freshly grated cheddar cheese

1 tbsp butter for greasing

⅓ cup freshly grated
   Parmesan cheese

salt and pepper

LAMB SAUCE

2 tbsp olive oil

1 large onion, sliced

2 celery stalks, sliced thinly

2 cups ground lamb

3 tbsp tomato paste

5½ oz/150 g bottled sun-dried
   tomatoes, drained and chopped

1 tsp dried oregano

1 tbsp red wine vinegar

⅝ cup chicken bouillon

salt and pepper

1 Put the eggplant slices into a strainer, sprinkle with salt and set aside for 45 minutes.

2 To make the lamb sauce, heat the oil in a pan over a low heat. Add the onion and celery and cook for 3–4 minutes. Add the lamb and cook, stirring frequently, until browned. Stir in the remaining sauce ingredients and season to taste. Bring to a boil and cook for 20 minutes.

3 Rinse the eggplant. Drain and pat dry on paper towels. Heat the oil in a skillet over a medium heat. Add the eggplant and cook for 4 minutes on each side. Remove and drain well.

4 Bring a large pan of lightly salted water to a boil over a medium heat. Add the pasta and cook until almost done. Drain thoroughly.

5 Gently heat the Bechamel Sauce (see page 98), stirring constantly. Stir in the cheddar cheese. Stir half of the cheese sauce into the pasta.

6 Layer the pasta, lamb sauce, and eggplant slices in a greased dish. Spread remaining cheese sauce over the top, then sprinkle with Parmesan cheese. Cook in a preheated oven at 375°F/190°C, for 25 minutes. Serve.

layered meat loaf

serves six

2 tbsp butter, plus extra for greasing

1 small onion, chopped finely

1 small red bell pepper, seeded
and chopped

1 garlic clove, chopped

4 cups ground beef

scant ½ cup fresh white
bread crumbs

½ tsp cayenne pepper

1 tbsp lemon juice

½ tsp grated lemon peel

2 tbsp chopped fresh parsley

¾ cup dried short pasta, such
as fusilli

1 cup Italian Cheese Sauce
(see page 7)

4 bay leaves

6 oz/175 g fatty bacon

salt and pepper

salad greens, to serve

1 Melt the butter in a pan over a medium heat. Add the onion and bell pepper and cook for 3 minutes. Stir in the garlic and cook for 1 minute.

2 Put the ground beef into a bowl and mash with a wooden spoon until sticky. Add the onion mixture, bread crumbs, cayenne pepper, lemon juice, lemon peel, and parsley. Season to taste with salt and pepper. Set aside.

3 Bring a large pan of lightly salted water to a boil over a medium heat. Add the pasta and cook for about 8–10 minutes, or until almost done. Drain thoroughly and stir into the Italian Cheese Sauce (see page 7).

4 Grease a 2-lb 4-oz/1-kg loaf pan and arrange the bay leaves in the bottom. Stretch the bacon slices with the back of a knife and use to line the bottom and sides of the pan. Spoon in half the meat mixture and level the surface. Cover with the pasta, then spoon in the remaining meat mixture. Level the top and cover with foil.

5 Cook the meat loaf in a preheated oven at 350°F/180°C, for 1 hour, or until the juices run clear when the point of a sharp knife is inserted into the center and the loaf has shrunk away from the sides of the pan. Pour off any fat and turn out the loaf onto a serving dish. Serve with salad greens.

meatballs in italian red wine sauce

serves four

⅔ cup milk

2 cups white bread crumbs

12 shallots, chopped

4 cups ground steak

1 tsp paprika

1 lb/450 g dried egg tagliarini

salt and pepper

fresh basil sprigs, to garnish

ITALIAN RED WINE SAUCE

2 tbsp butter

8 tbsp olive oil

3 cups sliced exotic mushrooms

¼ cup whole-wheat flour

⅞ cup beef bouillon

⅔ cup red wine

4 tomatoes, peeled and chopped

1 tbsp tomato paste

1 tsp brown sugar

1 tbsp finely chopped fresh basil

1 Put the bread crumbs into a bowl and pour over the milk. Let soak for 30 minutes.

2 Heat half the butter and half the oil in a pan over a low heat. Add the mushrooms and fry for 4 minutes. Stir in the flour and cook for 2 minutes. Add the bouillon and wine and cook for 15 minutes. Add the tomatoes, tomato paste, sugar, and basil. Season to taste with salt and pepper and cook for 30 minutes.

3 Mix the shallots, steak, and paprika with the bread crumbs and season. Shape into 14 meatballs.

4 Heat the remaining oil and the remaining butter in a skillet. Add the meatballs, and fry until browned. Transfer to a casserole dish, pour over sauce, cover and cook in a preheated oven, at 350°F/180°C, for 30 minutes.

5 Bring a large pan of lightly salted water to a boil over a medium heat. Add the pasta and cook for 8–10 minutes, or until done. Drain and transfer to a serving dish. Remove the casserole from the oven and pour the meatballs and sauce onto the pasta. Garnish with a basil sprig and serve.

tagliatelle with pumpkin & prosciutto

serves four

1 lb 2 oz/500 g pumpkin or
   butternut squash, peeled

2 tbsp olive oil

1 onion, chopped finely

2 garlic cloves, minced

4–6 tbsp chopped fresh parsley

pinch of freshly grated nutmeg

1¼ cups chicken or
   vegetable bouillon

4 oz/115 g prosciutto

9 oz/250 g dried tagliatelle

⅝ cup heavy cream

salt and pepper

freshly grated Parmesan cheese,
   to serve

1 Cut the pumpkin or butternut squash in half and scoop out the seeds with a spoon. Cut the pumpkin or squash into ½-inch/1-cm dice.

2 Heat the oil in a large pan over a low heat. Add the onion and garlic and cook for about 3 minutes, or until softened. Add half the parsley and cook for 1 minute.

3 Add the pumpkin pieces and cook for 2–3 minutes. Season to taste with salt, pepper, and nutmeg.

4 Add half the bouillon to the pan and bring to a boil over a medium heat. Cover and simmer for about 10 minutes, or until the pumpkin is tender. Add more bouillon if the pumpkin is becoming dry and looks as if it might burn.

5 Add the prosciutto to the pan and cook, stirring frequently, for an additional 2 minutes.

6 Meanwhile, bring a large pan of lightly salted water to a boil over a medium heat. Add the pasta and cook for 12 minutes, or until done. Drain the pasta thoroughly and transfer to a large, warmed serving dish.

7 Stir the cream into the pumpkin and ham mixture and heat through. Spoon over the pasta, then sprinkle over the remaining parsley. Serve with the grated Parmesan cheese separately.

97

stuffed cannelloni

serves four

8 dried cannelloni tubes

⅓ cup freshly grated
   Parmesan cheese

fresh herb sprigs, to garnish

FILLING

2 tbsp butter

1½ cups frozen spinach, thawed,
   drained, and chopped

½ cup ricotta cheese

⅓ cup freshly grated
   Parmesan cheese

¼ cup chopped ham

pinch of freshly grated nutmeg

2 tbsp heavy cream

2 eggs, beaten lightly

salt and pepper

BECHAMEL SAUCE

2 tbsp butter

scant ¼ cup all-purpose flour

1¼ cups milk

2 bay leaves

pinch of freshly grated nutmeg

1 To make the filling, melt the butter in a pan over a low heat. Add the spinach and cook for 2–3 minutes. Remove from the heat and stir in the ricotta and Parmesan cheeses, and the ham. Season with nutmeg, salt, and pepper. Beat in the cream and eggs to make a thick paste.

2 Bring a large pan of lightly salted water to a boil over a medium heat. Add the pasta and cook for 10–12 minutes, or until done. Drain the pasta thoroughly and let cool.

3 To make the sauce, melt the butter in a pan over a low heat. Stir in the flour and cook, stirring, for 1 minute. Gradually whisk in the milk. Add the bay leaves and simmer, whisking gently for 5 minutes. Add the nutmeg, salt and pepper. Remove from the heat and discard the bay leaves.

4 Spoon the filling into a pastry bag and use to fill the cannelloni.

5 Spoon a little sauce into the bottom of an ovenproof dish. Put the cannelloni in a single layer on the sauce, then pour over the remaining sauce. Sprinkle the Parmesan cheese over and cook in a preheated oven at 375°F/190°C, for 40–45 minutes. Garnish with fresh herb sprigs and serve immediately.

sicilian spaghetti

serves four

⅝ cup olive oil, plus extra
    for brushing

2 eggplant

3 cups ground beef

1 onion, chopped

2 garlic cloves, minced

2 tbsp tomato paste

14 oz/400 g canned
    chopped tomatoes

1 tsp Worcestershire sauce

1 tsp chopped fresh marjoram or
    oregano or ½ tsp dried marjoram
    or oregano

½ cup pitted ripe black olives, sliced

1 green, red, or yellow bell pepper,
    seeded and chopped

6 oz/175 g dried spaghetti

1 cup freshly grated
    Parmesan cheese

salt and pepper

1 Brush an 8-inch/20-cm loose-
bottomed round cake pan
with oil. Line the base with baking
parchment and brush with a little oil.

2 Slice the eggplant. Heat a little oil
in a pan over a low heat. Add the
eggplant, in batches, and cook until
browned on both sides. Add more oil,
as necessary. Drain on paper towels.

3 Put the beef, onion, and garlic in
a pan and cook over a medium
heat, stirring, until browned. Add the
tomato paste, tomatoes, Worcestershire
sauce, marjoram, and salt and pepper.
Simmer for 10 minutes. Add the olives
and pepper and cook for 10 minutes.

4 Bring a large pan of lightly salted
water to a boil over a medium
heat. Add the pasta and cook until
done. Drain the pasta thoroughly and
transfer to a large bowl. Add the meat
mixture and cheese and, using 2 forks,
toss together.

5 Arrange the eggplant slices over
the bottom and up the sides of
the pan. Add the pasta, then cover
with the rest of the eggplant. Cook in a
preheated oven at 400°F/200°C, for
40 minutes. Let stand for 5 minutes,
then invert onto a serving dish. Discard
the baking parchment and serve.

cannelloni

serves four

1 cup lean ground beef

1 large red onion, chopped finely

2½ cups white
    mushrooms, chopped

1 garlic clove, minced

½ tsp ground nutmeg

1 tsp dried mixed herbs

2 tbsp tomato paste

4 tbsp dry red wine

12 dried "quick cook"
    cannelloni tubes

salt and pepper

mixed salad, to serve

TOMATO SAUCE

1 red onion, chopped finely

1 large carrot, grated

1 celery stalk, chopped finely

1 bay leaf

⅔ cup dry red wine

400 g/14 oz canned
    chopped tomatoes

2 tbsp tomato paste

1 tsp superfine sugar

salt and pepper

TO GARNISH

¼ cup Parmesan cheese shavings

1 plum tomato

1 fresh basil sprig

1 Put the beef, onion, mushrooms, and garlic into a skillet and cook for 3–4 minutes. Stir in the nutmeg, herbs, seasoning, tomato paste, and wine. Simmer for 15–20 minutes. Let cool for 10 minutes.

2 Put the onion, carrot, celery, bay leaf, and wine into a pan. Bring to a boil over a low heat and cook for 5 minutes. Add the other sauce ingredients and simmer for 15 minutes. Remove the bay leaf and discard.

3 Spoon one-quarter of the sauce into the bottom of an ovenproof dish. Fill the cannelloni with the meat mixture and put on top of the sauce. Spoon over the remaining sauce. Cook in a preheated oven at 400°F/200°C, for 35–40 minutes. Garnish with the Parmesan cheese, plum tomato, and basil sprig. Serve immediately.

spaghetti bolognese

serves four

1 tbsp olive oil

1 onion, chopped finely

2 garlic cloves, chopped

1 carrot, chopped

1 celery stalk, chopped

¼ cup pancetta or lean bacon, diced

1½ cups lean ground beef

14 oz/400 g canned
   chopped tomatoes

2 tsp dried oregano

scant ½ cup red wine

2 tbsp tomato paste

salt and pepper

1 lb 7 oz/650 g fresh spaghetti or
   12 oz/350 g dried spaghetti

VARIATION

Try adding ¼ cup dried porcini,
soaked for 20 minutes in
2 tbsp of warm water,
to the bolognese sauce in
step 4, if you wish.

---

1 Heat the oil in a large skillet over a high heat. Add the onions and cook for 3 minutes.

2 Add the garlic, carrot, celery, and pancetta or bacon, and cook for about 3–4 minutes, or until just starting to brown.

3 Add the beef and cook over a high heat for 3 minutes, or until the meat has browned.

4 Stir in the tomatoes, oregano, and red wine and bring to a boil over a high heat. Reduce the heat and simmer for about 45 minutes.

5 Stir in the tomato paste and season with salt and pepper.

6 Bring a pan of lightly salted water to a boil over a medium heat. Add the pasta and cook for about 8–10 minutes, or until done. Drain.

7 Transfer the pasta to 4 serving plates and pour over the sauce. Toss to mix well and serve with Parmesan cheese, if you wish.

red spiced beef

serves four

1 lb 6 oz/625 g short loin or
  loin end steak

2 tbsp paprika

2–3 tsp mild chili powder

½ tsp salt

6 celery stalks

6 tbsp bouillon or water

2 tbsp tomato paste

2 tbsp honey

1 tbsp Worcestershire sauce

3 tbsp wine vinegar

2 tbsp corn oil

4 scallions, thinly sliced diagonally

4 tomatoes, peeled, seeded,
  and sliced

1–2 garlic cloves, minced

celery leaves, to garnish (optional)

cooked Chinese noodles, to serve

1 Cut the steak across the grain into narrow strips about ½-inch/1-cm thick and put into a bowl.

2 Mix the paprika, chili powder, and salt together. Add to the beef and mix until the meat is coated with the spices. Set the beef aside to marinate in the refrigerator for 30 minutes.

3 Cut the celery into 2-inch/5-cm lengths, then cut the lengths into strips about ¼-inch/5-mm thick.

4 Mix the bouillon, tomato paste, honey, Worcestershire sauce, and vinegar together and set aside.

5 Heat a wok over a high heat. Add the oil and when hot, add the scallion, celery, tomatoes, and garlic. Cook for 1 minute, then add the steak. Cook over a high heat for 3-4 minutes until the meat is sealed. Add the sauce and cook until coated and sizzling.

6 Garnish with celery leaves (if using) and serve with noodles.

spiced fried ground pork

serves four

2 tbsp corn oil

2 garlic cloves, chopped finely

3 shallots, chopped finely

2 tsp finely chopped fresh
  gingerroot

1 lb 2 oz/500 g lean ground pork

2 tbsp Thai fish sauce

1 tbsp dark soy sauce

1 tbsp red curry paste

4 dried kaffir lime leaves, crumbled

4 plum tomatoes, chopped

3 tbsp chopped fresh cilantro

salt and pepper

fresh cilantro leaves, to garnish

boiled fine egg noodles, to serve

1 Heat a wok over a high heat. Add the oil and when hot, add the garlic, shallots, and ginger. Cook for about 2 minutes, then stir in the pork and cook until golden brown.

2 Stir in the fish sauce, soy sauce, red curry paste, and lime leaves and cook for an additional 1–2 minutes over a high heat.

3 Add the chopped tomatoes and cook, stirring occasionally, for an additional 5–6 minutes.

4 Stir in the chopped cilantro and season to taste with salt and pepper. Pile boiled fine egg noodles onto 4 large, warmed serving plates and spoon over the spiced pork. Garnish with a few fresh cilantro leaves and serve immediately.

tagliatelle with meatballs

serves four

1 lb 2 oz/500 g lean ground beef

1 cup soft white bread crumbs

1 garlic clove, minced

2 tbsp chopped fresh parsley

1 tsp dried oregano

pinch of freshly grated nutmeg

¼ tsp ground coriander

⅔ cup freshly grated
    Parmesan cheese

2–3 tbsp milk

all-purpose flour, for dusting

3 tbsp olive oil

14 oz/400 g dried tagliatelle

2 tbsp butter, diced

salt and pepper

TOMATO SAUCE

3 tbsp olive oil

2 large onions, sliced

2 celery stalks, sliced thinly

2 garlic cloves, chopped

14 oz/400 g canned
    chopped tomatoes

⅔ cup sun-dried tomatoes in oil,
    drained and chopped

2 tbsp tomato paste

1 tbsp molasses sugar

⅔ cup white wine or water

1 To make the sauce, heat the oil in a skillet over a high heat. Add the onions and celery and cook until translucent. Add the garlic and cook for 1 minute. Stir in the tomatoes, tomato paste, sugar, and wine. Season to taste with salt and pepper. Bring to a boil and simmer for 10 minutes.

2 Meanwhile, break up the beef in a large bowl until it becomes a sticky paste. Stir in the bread crumbs, garlic, herbs, and spices. Stir in the Parmesan cheese and enough milk to make a firm paste. Lightly flour your hands, take large spoonfuls of the mixture, and shape it into 12 balls. Heat the oil in a skillet over a medium heat. Add the meatballs and cook for 5–6 minutes, or until browned.

3 Pour the tomato sauce over the meatballs. Reduce the heat, cover the pan, and simmer for 30 minutes, turning once or twice. Add a little extra water if the sauce is starting to become too dry.

4 Bring a large pan of lightly salted water to a boil over a medium heat. Add the pasta and cook for 8–10 minutes, or until done. Drain the pasta thoroughly, then transfer to a warmed serving dish, dot with the butter, and toss with 2 forks. Spoon meatballs and sauce over the pasta and transfer to 4 warmed serving plates. Serve immediately.

neapolitan veal chops with mascarpone

serves four

⅞ cup butter

4 x 9 oz/250 g veal chops, trimmed

1 large onion, sliced

2 apples, peeled, cored, and sliced

6 oz/175 g white mushrooms

1 tbsp chopped fresh tarragon

8 black peppercorns

1 tbsp sesame seeds

14 oz/400 g dried marille

scant ½ cup extra virgin olive oil

¾ cup mascarpone cheese, broken
   into small pieces

2 large beefsteak tomatoes, cut
   in half

leaves of 1 fresh basil sprig

salt and pepper

1 Melt 4 tablespoons of the butter in a skillet over a low heat. Cook the veal for 5 minutes on each side. Transfer to a dish and keep warm.

2 Put the onion and apples into the skillet and cook until lightly browned. Transfer to a dish, then put the veal on top and keep warm.

3 Melt the remaining butter in the skillet over a low heat. Add the mushrooms, tarragon, and peppercorns and cook for 3 minutes. Sprinkle over the sesame seeds.

4 Bring a large pan of lightly salted water to a boil over a medium heat. Add the pasta and cook for about 8–10 minutes, or until done. Drain the pasta thoroughly and transfer to a large ovenproof casserole dish

5 Top the pasta with the mascarpone and sprinkle over the oil. Put the onions, apples, and veal chops on top of the pasta. Spoon the mushrooms and peppercorns onto the chops, then arrange the tomatoes and

basil leaves around the edge and season to taste with salt and pepper. Cook in a preheated oven at 300°F/150°C, for about 5 minutes.

6 Remove from the oven and transfer to 4 serving plates. Serve.

fettuccine with veal in a rose petal sauce

serves four

1 lb/450 g dried fettuccine

6 tbsp olive oil

1 tsp chopped fresh oregano

1 tsp chopped fresh marjoram

¾ cup butter

1 lb/450 g veal fillet, sliced thinly

⅝ cup rose petal vinegar
    (see Cook's Tip)

⅝ cup fish bouillon

¼ cup grapefruit juice

¼ cup heavy cream

salt

TO GARNISH

12 pink grapefruit segments

12 pink peppercorns

rose petals, washed

COOK'S TIP

To make rose petal vinegar, infuse the rinsed petals of 8 pesticide-free roses in 150 ml/5 fl oz white wine vinegar for 48 hours.

1 Bring a large pan of lightly salted water to a boil over a medium heat. Add the pasta and cook for about 12 minutes, or until done. Drain the pasta thoroughly and transfer to a large, warmed serving dish, sprinkle over 2 tablespoons of the oil, the oregano, and marjoram.

2 Heat 4 tablespoons of the butter with the remaining oil in a large skillet over a low heat. Add the veal and cook for 6 minutes. Remove from the skillet and put on top of the pasta.

3 Add the vinegar and fish bouillon to the skillet and bring to a boil over a medium heat. Boil vigorously until reduced by two-thirds. Reduce the heat and add the grapefruit juice and cream. Simmer over a low heat for 4 minutes. Dice the remaining butter and add to the skillet, a piece at a time, whisking, until incorporated.

4 Pour the sauce around the veal, garnish with grapefruit segments, pink peppercorns, rose petals, then serve immediately.

creamed strips of sirloin with rigatoni

serves four

6 tbsp butter

1 lb/450 g sirloin steak, trimmed
and cut into thin strips

6 oz/175 g white mushrooms, sliced

1 tsp mustard

pinch of freshly grated gingerroot

2 tbsp dry sherry

⅝ cup heavy cream

1 lb/450 g dried rigatoni

2 fresh basil sprigs

8 tbsp butter

salt and pepper

4 slices hot toast, cut into triangles,
to serve

COOK'S TIP

Dried pasta will keep for up to
6 months. Keep it in the packet
and reseal it once you have
opened it, or transfer the pasta
to an airtight jar.

1 Melt the butter in a large skillet over a low heat. Add the steak and cook, stirring frequently, for about 6 minutes. Using a slotted spoon, transfer the steak to a large ovenproof dish and keep warm.

2 Add the sliced mushrooms to the skillet and cook for 2–3 minutes in the juices remaining in the skillet. Add the mustard, grated ginger, salt, and pepper. Cook for 2 minutes, then add the sherry and cream. Cook for an additional 3 minutes, then pour the cream sauce over the steak.

3 Cook the steak and cream mixture in a preheated oven at 375°F/190°C, for 10 minutes.

4 Meanwhile, bring a large pan of lightly salted water to a boil over a medium heat. Add the pasta and 1 of the basil sprigs and boil rapidly for 10 minutes, or until done. Drain the pasta thoroughly and transfer to a large, warmed serving plate. Toss the pasta with the butter and garnish with the other basil sprig.

5 Transfer the steak to 4 warmed serving plates and serve with the pasta and triangles of hot toast.

drunken noodles

serves four

6 oz/175 g rice stick noodles

2 tbsp vegetable oil

1 garlic clove, minced

2 small fresh green chiles, chopped

1 small onion, sliced thinly

⅛ cup lean ground pork or chicken

1 small green bell pepper, seeded
and chopped finely

4 kaffir lime leaves, shredded finely

1 tbsp dark soy sauce

1 tbsp light soy sauce

½ tsp sugar

1 tomato, cut into thin wedges

2 tbsp fresh sweet basil leaves,
shredded finely, to garnish

COOK'S TIP

Fresh kaffir lime leaves freeze
well, so if you buy more than
you need, simply tie them in a
tightly sealed plastic freezer bag
and freeze for up to 1 month.
They can be used straight from
the freezer.

1 Put the noodles in a bowl and pour over enough hot water to cover. Let soak for 15 minutes. Drain.

2 Heat a large wok over a high heat. Add the oil and when hot, add the garlic, chiles, and onion. Cook for 1 minute.

3 Stir in the pork and cook over a high heat for 1 minute, then add the bell pepper and continue cooking for an additional 2 minutes.

4 Stir in the lime leaves, soy sauces, and sugar. Add the noodles and tomato and toss to heat thoroughly.

5 Transfer to 4 large, warmed serving plates and sprinkle with the shredded basil leaves. Serve hot.

venison meatballs with kumquat sauce

serves four

2 cups lean ground venison

1 small leek, chopped finely

1 medium carrot, grated finely

½ tsp ground nutmeg

1 medium egg white, beaten lightly

salt and pepper

SAUCE

3½ oz/100 g kumquats

1 tbsp superfine sugar

⅔ cup water

4 tbsp dry sherry

1 tsp cornstarch

TO SERVE

freshly cooked pasta or noodles

freshly cooked vegetables

1 Put the venison into a mixing bowl together with the leek, carrot, seasoning, and nutmeg. Add the egg white and bind the ingredients together with your hands until the mixture is well molded and firm.

2 Divide the mixture into 16 equal portions. Using your fingers, form each portion into a small round ball.

3 Bring a large pan of water to a boil over a medium heat. Arrange the meatballs on a layer of baking parchment in a steamer and put over the boiling water. Cover and steam for 10 minutes, or until cooked through.

4 Meanwhile, wash and thinly slice the kumquats. Put them into a pan with the sugar and water and bring to a boil over a low heat. Cook for 2–3 minutes, or until tender.

5 Blend the sherry and cornstarch together and add to the pan. Heat through, stirring, until the kumquat sauce thickens. Season to taste.

6 Drain the meatballs and transfer to a serving plate. Spoon over the sauce and serve with freshly cooked pasta and vegetables.

113

pasta & pork in cream sauce

serves four

1 lb/450 g pork tenderloin,
   sliced thinly

4 tbsp olive oil

225 g/8 oz white mushrooms, sliced

⅞ cup Italian Red Wine Sauce
   (see page 96)

1 tbsp lemon juice

pinch of saffron

3 cups dried orecchioni

4 tbsp heavy cream

12 quail eggs (see Cook's Tip)

salt

COOK'S TIP

In this recipe, the quail eggs are soft-cooked. As they are extremely difficult to shell when warm, it is important that they are thoroughly cooled first. Otherwise, they will break up unattractively.

1 Put the pork slices between 2 sheets of cling film and pound until wafer thin, then cut into strips.

2 Heat the oil in a large skillet over a medium heat. Add the pork slices and cook for 5 minutes. Add the mushrooms and cook for an additional 2 minutes.

3 Pour over the Italian Red Wine Sauce (see page 96), reduce the heat and simmer gently for 20 minutes.

4 Meanwhile, bring a large pan of lightly salted water to a boil over a medium heat. Add the lemon juice, saffron, and pasta and cook for about 8–10 minutes, or until done. Drain the pasta thoroughly and keep warm.

5 Stir the cream into the pan with the pork and heat gently for a few minutes.

6 Boil the eggs for 3 minutes in a small pan of boiling water. Cool in cold water and remove the shells.

7 Transfer the pasta to a large, warmed serving plate, top with the pork and the sauce, and garnish with the eggs. Serve immediately.

broiled chicken with lemon & honey

serves four

4 boneless chicken breasts (about
   4¼ oz/125 g each)
2 tbsp honey
1 tbsp dark soy sauce
1 tsp finely grated lemon peel
1 tbsp lemon juice
salt and pepper
NOODLES
8 oz/225 g rice noodles
2 tsp sesame oil
1 tbsp sesame seeds
1 tsp finely grated lemon peel
finely grated lemon peel, to garnish

1 Using a sharp knife, skin and trim
the chicken breasts to remove any
excess fat, then wash in cold water
and pat them dry on paper towels.
Score the chicken breasts with a criss-
cross pattern on both sides (making
sure that you do not cut all the way
through the meat).

2 Mix the honey, soy sauce, lemon
peel, and juice together in a small
bowl, then season well with pepper.

3 Arrange the chicken breasts on a
broiler rack so they do not overlap
and brush with half the honey mixture.
Cook under a preheated medium-hot
broiler for 10 minutes, turn over, then
brush with the remaining mixture.
Cook for another 8–10 minutes, or
until cooked through.

4 Prepare the noodles according to
the package instructions. Drain
well and pile into a warmed serving
bowl. Mix the noodles with the sesame
oil, sesame seeds, and lemon peel.
Season and keep warm.

5 Drain the chicken and transfer to
4 serving plates with a mound of
noodles and garnish with lemon peel.
Serve immediately.

rice noodles with chicken

serves four

7 oz/200 g rice stick noodles

1 tbsp corn oil

1 garlic clove, chopped finely

¾-inch/2-cm piece of fresh
     gingerroot, chopped finely

4 scallions, chopped

1 fresh red bird-eye chile, seeded
     and sliced

10½ oz/300 g skinless, boneless
     chicken, chopped finely

2 chicken livers, chopped finely

1 celery stalk, sliced thinly

1 carrot, cut into fine batons

10½ oz/300 g shredded
     Napa cabbage

4 tbsp lime juice

2 tbsp Thai fish sauce

1 tbsp soy sauce

2 tbsp shredded fresh mint

slices of pickled garlic

1 fresh mint sprig, to garnish

1 Put the noodles into a bowl and
pour over enough hot water to
cover. Let soak for 15 minutes. Drain.

2 Heat the oil in a large skillet over
a high heat. Add the garlic,
ginger, scallions, and chile and cook for

about 1 minute. Stir in the chicken
and chicken livers, then cook for
2–3 minutes, until starting to brown.

3 Stir in the celery and carrot and
cook for 2 minutes to soften. Add
the Napa cabbage, then stir in the lime
juice, fish sauce, and soy sauce.

4 Add the cooked noodles and stir
to heat through thoroughly.
Sprinkle with shredded mint and
pickled garlic. Garnish with a mint
sprig and serve immediately.

egg noodles with beef & pasta

serves four

10 oz/285 g egg noodles

3 tbsp walnut oil

1-inch/2.5-cm piece fresh
   gingerroot, cut into thin strips

5 scallions, shredded finely

2 garlic cloves, chopped finely

1 red bell pepper, seeded and
   sliced thinly

3½ oz/100 g white mushrooms,
   sliced thinly

12 oz/350 g fillet steak, cut into
   thin strips

1 tbsp cornstarch

5 tbsp dry sherry

3 tbsp soy sauce

1 tsp soft brown sugar

1 cup bean sprouts

1 tbsp sesame oil

salt and pepper

scallion strips, to garnish

1 Bring a large pan of water to a boil over a medium heat. Add the noodles and cook according to the

package instructions. Drain the noodles thoroughly and set aside.

2 Heat a large wok over a high heat. Add the walnut oil and when hot, add the ginger, scallions, and garlic and cook for 45 seconds. Add the bell pepper, mushrooms, and steak and cook for 4 minutes. Season to taste with salt and pepper.

3 Mix the cornstarch, sherry, and soy sauce together in a small pitcher to form a paste, then pour into the wok. Sprinkle over the brown sugar and cook all of the ingredients for an additional 2 minutes.

4 Add the bean sprouts, drained noodles, and sesame oil to the wok, stir and toss together for 1 minute. Transfer to 4 bowls, garnish with scallion strips and serve.

COOK'S TIP

If you do not have a wok, you could prepare this dish in a skillet. However, a wok is preferable, as the round bottom ensures an even distribution of heat and it is easier to keep stirring and tossing the contents when cooking.

lemon chicken conchiglie

serves four

8 chicken pieces (about
4 oz/115 g each)

4 tbsp butter, melted

4 tbsp mild mustard (see Cook's Tip)

2 tbsp lemon juice

1 tbsp brown sugar

1 tsp paprika

3 tbsp poppy seeds

3½ cups fresh pasta shells

1 tbsp olive oil

salt and pepper

COOK'S TIP

Dijon is the type of mustard
most often used in cooking, as it
has a clean and only mildly spicy
flavor. German mustard has a
sweet-sour taste, with Bavarian
mustard being slightly sweeter.
American mustard is mild
and sweet.

1 Arrange the chicken pieces,
smooth-side down, in a single
layer in a large ovenproof dish.

2 Mix the butter, mustard, lemon
juice, sugar, and paprika together
in a bowl and season to taste with salt
and pepper. Brush the mixture over the
upper surfaces of the chicken pieces
and cook in a preheated oven at
400°F/200°C, for 15 minutes.

3 Remove the dish from the oven
and, using tongs, carefully turn
over the chicken pieces. Coat the upper
surfaces of the chicken with the
remaining mustard mixture, then
sprinkle with poppy seeds. Return to
the oven for an additional 15 minutes.

4 Meanwhile, bring a large pan of
lightly salted water to a boil over
a medium heat. Add the pasta shells
and oil and cook until done.

5 Drain the pasta and arrange in a
large, warmed serving dish. Top
with the chicken, pour over the sauce
and serve immediately.

chicken breasts filled with jumbo shrimp

serves four

4 x 7 oz/200 g chicken
   breasts, trimmed
4 oz/115 g large spinach leaves,
   trimmed and blanched in hot
   salted water
4 slices of prosciutto
12–16 raw jumbo shrimp, shelled
   and deveined
1 lb/450 g dried tagliatelle
1 tbsp olive oil
4 tbsp butter, plus extra for greasing
3 leeks, shredded
1 large carrot, grated
⅝ cup thick mayonnaise
2 large, cooked beet
salt

1 Grease 4 large pieces of foil
   and set aside. Put each breast
between 2 pieces of baking parchment
and pound with a rolling pin to flatten.

2 Divide half the spinach and put
   on top of the chicken breasts, add
a slice of ham to each and top with
more spinach. Put 3–4 shrimp on top.
Fold the pointed end of the breast over
the shrimp, then fold over again to
form a parcel. Wrap in foil, then put
onto a cookie sheet and cook in a
preheated oven at 400°F/200°C, for
about 20 minutes.

3 Meanwhile, bring a pan of lightly
   salted water to a boil over a
medium heat. Add the pasta and cook
until done. Drain the pasta thoroughly
and transfer to a large serving dish.

4 Melt the butter in a skillet over a
   low heat. Add the leeks and
carrots and cook for 3 minutes, then
transfer to the center of the pasta.

5 Put the mayonnaise and 1 beet
   into a food processor or blender
and process until smooth. Rub through
a strainer, then pour around the pasta
and vegetables.

6 Cut the remaining beet into
   diamond shapes and put neatly
around the mayonnaise. Remove the
foil from the chicken and, using a sharp
knife, cut the breasts into thin slices.
Arrange the slices on top of the pasta
and vegetables, then serve.

chicken & ham lasagna

serves four

1 tbsp butter for greasing

14 sheets precooked lasagna

3¾ cups Bechamel Sauce
   (see page 98)

1 cup freshly grated
   Parmesan cheese

CHICKEN & EXOTIC

MUSHROOM SAUCE

2 tbsp olive oil

2 garlic cloves, minced

1 large onion, chopped finely

3½ cups sliced exotic mushrooms

1⅜ cups ground chicken

3 oz/85 g chicken livers,
   chopped finely

4 oz/115 g prosciutto, diced

⅔ cup Marsala wine

10 oz/280 g canned
   chopped tomatoes

1 tbsp chopped fresh basil leaves

2 tbsp tomato paste

salt and pepper

1 To make the chicken and exotic mushroom sauce, heat the oil in a large pan over a low heat. Add the garlic, onion, and mushrooms. Cook, stirring frequently, for 6 minutes.

2 Add the ground chicken, chicken livers, and prosciutto. Cook, stirring frequently, for 12 minutes, or until the meat has browned.

3 Stir the Marsala, tomatoes, basil, and tomato paste and cook for about 4 minutes. Season to taste with salt and pepper, cover, and simmer for 30 minutes. Uncover, stir thoroughly, and simmer for 15 minutes.

4 Grease a casserole with butter. Arrange sheets of lasagna over the bottom of the dish, spoon a layer of the chicken and mushroom sauce, then spoon over a layer of Bechamel Sauce (see page 98). Put another layer of lasagna on top and repeat the process twice, finishing with a layer of Bechamel Sauce. Sprinkle over the cheese and cook in a preheated oven at 375°F/190°C, for 35 minutes, or until golden and bubbling, then serve.

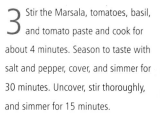

chicken & spinach lasagna

serves four

2 cups frozen chopped spinach,
  thawed, and drained

½ tsp ground nutmeg

1 lb/450 g lean, cooked chicken
  meat, skinned and diced

4 sheets precooked lasagna verde

1½ tbsp cornstarch

1¾ cups skim milk

scant ¾ cup freshly grated
  Parmesan cheese

salt and pepper

TOMATO SAUCE

14 oz/400 g canned
  chopped tomatoes

1 onion, chopped finely

1 garlic clove, minced

⅔ cup white wine

3 tbsp tomato paste

1 tsp dried oregano

1 To make the tomato sauce, put the tomatoes into a pan and stir in the onion, garlic, wine, tomato paste, and oregano. Bring to a boil over a low heat and simmer gently for 20 minutes until thick. Season well.

2 Drain the spinach again and spread it out on paper towels to make sure that as much water as possible is removed. Layer the spinach in the bottom of a large ovenproof dish, then sprinkle with ground nutmeg and season to taste with salt and pepper.

3 Arrange the diced chicken over the spinach and spoon over the tomato sauce. Arrange the sheets of lasagna over the tomato sauce.

4 Blend the cornstarch with a little of the milk to make a smooth paste. Pour the remaining milk into a pan and stir in the paste. Heat gently for 2–3 minutes, stirring, until the sauce thickens. Season well.

5 Spoon the sauce over the lasagna and transfer the dish to a cookie sheet. Sprinkle the grated cheese over the sauce and cook in a preheated oven at 400°F/200°C, for 25 minutes, or until golden, then serve.

pasta with chicken sauce

serves four

9 oz/250 g fresh green tagliatelle

1 tbsp olive oil

salt and pepper

fresh basil leaves, to garnish

TOMATO SAUCE

2 tbsp olive oil

1 small onion, chopped

1 garlic clove, chopped

14 oz/400 g canned
    chopped tomatoes

2 tbsp chopped fresh parsley

1 tsp dried oregano

2 bay leaves

2 tbsp tomato paste

1 tsp sugar

CHICKEN SAUCE

4 tbsp unsalted butter

14 oz/400 g boned chicken breasts,
    skinned and cut into thin strips

¾ cup blanched almonds

1¼ cups heavy cream

salt and pepper

1 To make the tomato sauce, heat the oil in a pan over a medium heat. Add the onion and cook until translucent. Add the garlic and cook for 1 minute. Stir in the tomatoes, parsley, oregano, bay leaves, tomato paste, and sugar. Season to taste with salt and pepper, bring to a boil and simmer, uncovered, for 15–20 minutes, or until reduced by half. Remove the pan from the heat and discard the bay leaves.

2 To make the chicken sauce, melt the butter in a skillet over a medium heat. Add the chicken and almonds and cook for 5–6 minutes, or until the chicken is cooked through.

3 Meanwhile, bring the cream to a boil in a small pan over a low heat and boil for about 10 minutes, or until reduced by almost half. Pour the cream over the chicken and almonds, stir and season to taste with salt and pepper. Set aside and keep warm.

4 Bring a large pan of lightly salted water to a boil over a medium heat. Add the pasta and oil and cook for 8–10 minutes, or until done. Drain the pasta and transfer to a warmed serving dish. Spoon over the tomato sauce and arrange the chicken sauce down the center. Garnish with the basil leaves and serve immediately.

chicken & lobster on penne

serves six

1 tbsp butter for greasing

6 chicken breasts portions

1 lb/450 g dried penne

2–3 tbsp extra virgin olive oil

1 cup grated Parmesan cheese

salt

fresh parsley leaves, to garnish

FILLING

4 oz/115 g lobster meat, chopped

2 shallots, chopped very finely

2 figs, chopped

1 tbsp Marsala wine

2 tbsp bread crumbs

1 large egg, beaten

salt and pepper

1 Grease 6 pieces of foil large enough to enclose each chicken breast and grease a cookie sheet.

2 Put all the filling ingredients into a mixing bowl and blend together thoroughly with a wooden spoon.

3 Cut a pocket in each chicken breast with a sharp knife and fill with the lobster mixture. Wrap each chicken breast in a piece of foil, then put the parcels onto the prepared cookie sheet and cook in a preheated oven at 400°F/200°C, for 30 minutes.

4 Meanwhile, bring a large pan of lightly salted water to a boil over a medium heat. Add the pasta and cook for about 10 minutes, or until done. Drain the pasta thoroughly and transfer to a large, warmed serving plate. Sprinkle over the oil and the grated Parmesan cheese, set aside, and keep warm.

5 Carefully remove the foil from around the chicken breasts. Slice the breasts very thinly, arrange over the pasta, and garnish with fresh parsley leaves. Serve immediately.

chicken tortellini

serves four

4 oz/115 g boned chicken
   breast, skinned

2 oz/55 g prosciutto

2 tbsp cooked spinach, well drained

1 tbsp finely chopped onion

2 tbsp freshly grated Parmesan cheese

pinch of ground allspice

1 egg, beaten

1 lb/450 g Homemade Pasta Dough
   (see page 50)

all-purpose flour, for dusting

salt and pepper

2 tbsp chopped fresh parsley,
   to garnish

SAUCE

1 cup light cream

2 garlic cloves, minced

⅔ cup white mushrooms,
   sliced thinly

4 tbsp freshly grated
   Parmesan cheese

1 Bring a pan of salted water to a boil over a medium heat. Add the chicken and cook for 10 minutes. Let cool slightly, then put into a blender, with the prosciutto, spinach, and onion and process until finely chopped. Stir in 2 tablespoons of the Parmesan cheese, the allspice, and beaten egg, and season to taste with salt and pepper.

2 Roll out the pasta dough thinly on a lightly floured counter and cut into 1½–2-inch/4–5-cm circles.

3 Put ½ tsp of the filling in the center of each circle. Fold the

pieces in half and press the edges to seal. Wrap each piece around your finger, cross over the ends and curl the rest of the dough backward to make a navel shape. Re-roll the trimmings and repeat until all the dough is used up.

4 Bring a large pan of lightly salted water to a boil over a medium heat. Add the tortellini, in batches, and cook for 5 minutes. Drain thoroughly and transfer to a serving dish.

5 To make the sauce, put the cream and garlic into a small pan and bring to a boil over a low heat, then simmer for 3 minutes. Add the mushrooms and half the Parmesan cheese, season and simmer for 2–3 minutes. Pour the sauce over the tortellini, sprinkle over the remaining Parmesan cheese, garnish with the chopped parsley and serve.

chicken with orange sauce

serves four

2 tbsp canola oil

2 tbsp olive oil

4 x 8 oz/225 g chicken breasts

⅔ cup brandy

2 tbsp all-purpose flour

⅔ cup freshly squeezed orange juice

¼ cup zucchini, cut into
thin batons

¼ cup red bell pepper, cut into
thin batons

¼ cup leek, shredded finely

14 oz/400 g dried
whole-wheat spaghetti

3 large oranges, peeled and cut
into segments

peel of 1 orange, cut into very
fine strips

2 tbsp chopped fresh tarragon

⅔ cup ricotta cheese

salt and pepper

fresh tarragon leaves, to garnish

1 Heat the canola oil and 1 tablespoon of the olive oil in a skillet over a fairly high heat. Add the chicken and cook until golden brown. Add the brandy and cook for about 3 minutes. Sprinkle in the flour and cook, stirring constantly, for 2 minutes.

2 Reduce the heat and add the orange juice, zucchini, red bell pepper, and leek. Season to taste with salt and pepper. Simmer for 5 minutes, or until the sauce has thickened.

3 Meanwhile, bring a pan of lightly salted water to a boil over a medium heat. Add the pasta and cook for 10 minutes, or until done. Drain the pasta thoroughly, transfer to a large, warmed serving dish and drizzle over the remaining oil.

4 Add half the orange segments, half the orange peel, the tarragon, and ricotta cheese to the sauce in the skillet and cook for about 3 minutes.

5 Put the chicken on top of the pasta, pour over a little sauce, garnish with the remaining orange segments, peel, and tarragon. Serve immediately with any extra sauce.

filipino chicken

serves four

1 can lemonade or lime-and-
    lemonade

2 tbsp gin

4 tbsp tomato catsup

2 tsp garlic salt

2 tsp Worcestershire sauce

4 lean chicken breasts

salt and pepper

TO SERVE

cooked thread egg noodles

1 fresh green chile, chopped finely

2 scallions, sliced

1 Mix the lemonade or lime-and-lemonade, gin, tomato catsup, garlic salt, and Worcestershire sauce together in a large non-porous dish. Season to taste with salt and pepper.

2 Put the chicken pieces into the dish pour over the gin mixture, ensure that the chicken is covered.

3 Let the chicken marinate in the refrigerator for 2 hours, then remove and let stand, covered, at room temperature for 30 minutes.

4 Put the chicken pieces over a medium-hot barbecue grill, and cook for 20 minutes, turning once, halfway through the cooking time.

5 Remove the cooked chicken from the barbecue grill and let rest for 3–4 minutes before serving.

6 Serve with cooked egg noodles, tossed with a little green chile and sliced scallions.

breast of pheasant lasagna

serves four

8 oz/225 g pork fat, diced

2 tbsp butter

16 pearl onions

8 large pheasant breasts,
   sliced thinly

scant ¼ cup all-purpose flour

2½ cups chicken bouillon

1 bouquet garni

1 lb/450 g fresh peas, shelled

1 tbsp butter for greasing

14 sheets precooked lasagna

3½ cups Bechamel Sauce
   (see page 98)

¾ cup freshly grated
   mozzarella cheese

salt

1 Bring a large pan of lightly salted water to a boil over a medium heat. Add the pork fat and simmer gently for 3 minutes, then drain, and pat dry on paper towels.

2 Melt the butter in a large skillet over a low heat. Add the dry pork fat and pearl onions to the skillet and cook, stirring constantly, for about 3 minutes, or until the fat and onions are lightly browned.

3 Remove the pork fat and onions from the skillet and set aside. Add the pheasant slices and cook over a low heat until browned all over. Transfer to an ovenproof dish.

4 Stir the flour into the skillet and cook until just brown. Blend in the bouillon, then pour the mixture over the pheasant. Add the bouquet garni, and cook in a preheated oven at 400°F/200°C, for 5 minutes. Remove the bouquet garni. Add the onions, pork fat, and peas, and return to the oven for 10 minutes.

5 Put the pheasant and pork fat into a food processor and chop finely.

6 Reduce the oven temperature to 375°F/190°C. Grease an ovenproof dish with butter. Layer the lasagna, pheasant sauce, and Bechamel Sauce (see page 98) in the dish, ending with Bechamel Sauce. Sprinkle over the cheese and cook for 30 minutes. Garnish with parsley and serve with baby onions and peas.

braised garlic chicken

serves four

4 garlic cloves, chopped

4 shallots, chopped

2 small fresh red chiles, seeded
and chopped

1 lemongrass stalk, chopped finely

1 tbsp chopped fresh cilantro

1 tsp shrimp paste

½ tsp ground cinnamon

1 tbsp tamarind paste

2 tbsp vegetable oil

8 chicken pieces, such as drumsticks
or thighs

1¼ cups chicken bouillon

1 tbsp Thai fish sauce

1 tbsp smooth peanut butter

4 tbsp toasted peanuts, chopped

salt and pepper

TO SERVE

stir-fried vegetables

boiled noodles

1 Put the garlic, shallots, chiles, lemongrass, cilantro, and shrimp paste into a mortar and pound with a pestle to an almost smooth paste. Stir in the cinnamon and tamarind paste.

2 Heat the oil in a skillet over a medium heat. Add the chicken pieces, turning frequently, until golden brown on all sides. Remove from the skillet with a slotted spoon and keep hot. Tip away any excess fat.

3 Add the garlic paste to the skillet and cook over a medium heat, stirring constantly, until lightly browned. Stir in the bouillon and return the chicken to the skillet.

4 Bring to a boil over a medium heat. Cover tightly, reduce the heat, and simmer, stirring occasionally, for 25–30 minutes, or until the chicken is tender and thoroughly cooked. Stir in the fish sauce and peanut butter and simmer for an additional 10 minutes.

5 Season to taste with salt and pepper and sprinkle the toasted peanuts over the chicken. Serve immediately with a selection of stir-fried vegetables and boiled noodles.

chicken with vegetables

serves four

4 part boned chicken breasts

2 tbsp butter

2 tbsp olive oil

1 large onion, chopped finely

2 garlic cloves, minced

2 bell peppers, red, yellow or green,
  seeded and cut into large pieces

8 oz/225 g large closed cup
  mushrooms, sliced or cut
  into fourths

6 oz/175 g tomatoes, peeled,
  and halved

⅔ cup dry white wine

¾–1 cup pitted green olives

4–6 tbsp heavy cream

salt and pepper

12 oz/350 g freshly cooked pasta

chopped fresh parsley, to garnish

1 Season the chicken with salt and pepper. Heat the oil and butter in a skillet over a medium heat. Add the chicken and cook until browned. Remove the chicken from the pan.

2 Add the onion and garlic to the skillet and cook gently until just softened. Add the bell peppers and cook for a few minutes.

3 Add the tomatoes and plenty of seasoning to the pan, then transfer the vegetable mixture to an ovenproof casserole. Put the chicken onto the bed of vegetables.

4 Add the wine to the skillet and bring to a boil over a medium heat. Pour the wine over the chicken, cover and cook in a preheated oven at 350°F/180°C, for 50 minutes.

5 Add the olives to the chicken, mix lightly, then pour on the cream. Re-cover the casserole and return to the oven for 10–20 minutes, or until the chicken is very tender.

6 Adjust the seasoning and serve the chicken, surrounded by the vegetables and sauce, with freshly cooked pasta. Garnish with chopped parsley and serve immediately.

slices of duck with pasta

serves four

4 x 10½ oz/275 g boned breasts
of duckling

2 tbsp butter

¼ cup finely chopped carrots

¼ cup finely chopped shallots

1 tbsp lemon juice

⅔ cup meat bouillon

4 tbsp honey

1 cup fresh or frozen raspberries,
thawed if frozen

¼ cup all-purpose flour

1 tbsp Worcestershire sauce

14 oz/400 g fresh linguine

salt and pepper

TO GARNISH

fresh raspberries

4 fresh Italian parsley sprigs

1 Trim and score the duck breasts. Season well. Melt the butter in a skillet over a low heat. Add the duck and cook until lightly colored.

2 Add the carrots, shallots, lemon juice, and half the bouillon and simmer over a low heat for 1 minute. Stir in half the honey and half the raspberries. Sprinkle over half the flour and cook, stirring constantly, for 3 minutes. Season with pepper to taste and add the Worcestershire sauce.

3 Stir in the remaining bouillon and cook for 1 minute. Stir in the remaining honey and remaining raspberries and sprinkle over the remaining flour. Cook for an additional 3 minutes.

4 Remove the duck breasts from the skillet, but let the sauce simmer over a very low heat.

5 Meanwhile, bring a large pan of lightly salted water to a boil over a medium heat. Add the pasta and cook until done. Drain and transfer to 4 large, warmed serving plates.

6 Slice the duck breast lengthwise into ¼-inch/5-mm thick pieces. Pour a little sauce over the pasta and arrange the sliced duck in a fan shape on top of it. Garnish with a few fresh raspberries and Italian parsley sprigs, then serve immediately.

Fish & Seafood

Pasta is a natural partner for fish and seafood. Both are cooked quickly to preserve their flavor and texture, they are packed full of nutritional goodness, and the varieties available are almost infinite. These recipes feature exciting and tempting ways of cooking fish and meat to make a range of satisfying meals that are typically Italian. Fish is one of the most important food sources in Italy. The fish markets there are fascinating, with a huge variety of local fish on display. Fresh or frozen imported fish of all kinds from the Mediterranean are appearing increasingly in fishmongers and supermarkets, giving us access to dishes that were once only the preserve of the Italians. This chapter contains a wealth of fish and seafood recipes to suit all occasions.

steamed pasta pudding

serves four

1 cup dried short-cut macaroni or
    other short pasta

1 tbsp butter, plus extra for greasing

1 lb/450 g white fish fillets, such as
    cod or haddock

2–3 fresh parsley sprigs

6 black peppercorns

½ cup heavy cream

2 eggs, separated

2 tbsp chopped fresh dill or parsley

pinch of freshly grated nutmeg

⅔ cup freshly grated
    Parmesan cheese

salt and pepper

fresh dill or parsley sprigs,
    to garnish

Tomato Sauce, to serve
    (see page 126)

1 Bring a large pan of lightly salted water to a boil. Add the pasta and cook until done. Drain the pasta thoroughly, then return to the pan and add the butter. Cover and keep warm.

2 Put the fish into a skillet. Add the parsley sprigs, peppercorns, and enough water to cover. Bring to a boil over a medium heat, cover and simmer for 10 minutes. Lift out the fish and let cool. Set aside the cooking liquid.

3 Skin the fish and cut into bite-size pieces. Put the pasta into a bowl. Mix the cream, egg yolks, chopped dill, nutmeg, and cheese together, then pour into the pasta and mix. Spoon in the fish without breaking it. Add enough of the reserved cooking liquid to make a moist, but firm mixture. Whisk the egg whites until stiff, then fold into the mixture.

4 Grease a heatproof bowl and spoon in the fish mixture to within 1½ inches/4 cm of the rim. Cover with greased baking parchment and foil and tie securely with string.

5 Stand the bowl on a trivet in a pan. Add enough boiling water to reach halfway up the sides. Cover and steam for 1½ hours.

6 Invert the pudding onto a serving plate. Pour over a little Tomato Sauce (see page 126). Garnish with dill and serve with the remaining sauce.

baked seafood & macaroni with fennel

serves four

3 cups dried short-cut macaroni

1 tbsp olive oil, plus extra for
    brushing

6 tbsp butter, plus extra for
    greasing

2 small fennel bulbs, thinly sliced
    and fronds reserved

6 oz mushrooms, thinly sliced

6 oz peeled, cooked shrimp

pinch of cayenne pepper

1¼ cups Béchamel Sauce (see
    Cook's Tip)

⅔ cup freshly grated Parmesan
    cheese

2 large tomatoes, sliced

1 tsp dried oregano

salt and pepper

1 Bring a pan of salted water to a
boil. Add the pasta and oil and
cook until tender, but still firm to the
bite. Drain and return to the pan. Add
2 tbsp of butter, then cover and shake
the pan. Keep warm.

2 Melt the remaining butter in a
pan. Fry the fennel for 3–4
minutes. Stir in the mushrooms and
cook for an additional 2 minutes. Stir in
the shrimp, then remove from the heat.

3 Stir the cayenne pepper and
shrimp mixture into the Béchamel
sauce. Pour into a greased ovenproof
dish and spread evenly. Sprinkle over
the Parmesan cheese and arrange the
tomato slices in a ring around the
edge. Brush the tomatoes with olive oil
and sprinkle over the oregano.

4 Bake in a preheated oven at
350°F for 25 minutes, until
golden brown. Serve immediately.

COOK'S TIP

For Béchamel sauce, melt 2 tbsp
butter. Stir in 1/4 cup flour. Cook,
stirring, for 2 minutes. Gradually,
stir in 11/4 cups warm milk. Add
2 tbsp finely chopped onion, 5
white peppercorns, and 2 parsley
sprigs, then season with salt,
dried thyme, and grated nutmeg.
Simmer, stirring, for 15 minutes.
Strain before using.

trout with smoked bacon

serves four

1 tbsp butter for greasing

4 whole trout, 9½ oz/275 g each,
   gutted and cleaned

12 canned anchovy fillets in oil,
   drained and chopped

2 apples, peeled, cored, and sliced

4 fresh mint sprigs

juice of 1 lemon

12 slices smoked fatty bacon

1 lb/450 g dried tagliatelle

salt and pepper

TO GARNISH

2 apples, cored and sliced

4 fresh mint sprigs

1 Grease a deep cookie sheet with the butter.

2 Open up the cavities of each trout and rinse with warm salt water.

3 Season each cavity with salt and pepper. Divide the anchovies, sliced apples, and mint sprigs among the cavities. Sprinkle the lemon juice into each cavity.

4 Carefully cover the whole of eac trout, except the head and tail, with 3 slices of smoked bacon in a spiral shape.

5 Arrange the trout on the cookie sheet with the loose ends of bacon tucked underneath. Season wit pepper and cook in a preheated oven at 400°F/200°C, for 20 minutes, turning the trout over after 10 minute

6 Meanwhile, bring a large pan of lightly salted water to a boil over a medium heat. Add the pasta and cook for about 12 minutes, or un done. Drain the pasta thoroughly and transfer to 4 warmed serving plates.

7 Remove the trout from the oven and arrange on the pasta. Garni with sliced apples and fresh mint sprigs, then serve immediately.

sea bass with macaroni & olive sauce

serves four

2 tbsp butter

4 shallots, chopped

2 tbsp capers

1 cup pitted green olives, chopped

4 tbsp balsamic vinegar

1¼ cups fish bouillon

1¼ cups heavy cream

juice of 1 lemon

4 cups dried macaroni

8 x 4 oz/115 g sea bass medallions

salt and pepper

mixture of lemon slices, shredded
   leek, and shredded carrot,
   to garnish

1 To make the sauce, melt the butter in a skillet over a low heat. Add the shallots and cook for 4 minutes. Add the capers and olives and cook for an additional 3 minutes.

2 Stir in the balsamic vinegar and fish bouillon, bring to a boil over a low heat and reduce by half. Add the cream, stirring, and reduce again by half. Season to taste with salt and pepper and stir in the lemon juice. Remove the pan from the heat, set aside and keep warm.

3 Bring a large pan of lightly salted water to a boil over a medium heat. Add the pasta and cook for about 12 minutes, or until done.

4 Cook the sea bass medallions under a preheated hot broiler for 3–4 minutes on each side, until cooked through, do not overcook.

5 Drain the pasta and transfer to 4 large, warmed serving dishes. Top the pasta with the fish medallions and pour over the olive sauce. Garnish with lemon slices, shredded leek, and shredded carrot. Serve immediately.

spaghetti al tonno

serves four

7 oz/200 g canned tuna, drained

2 oz/55 g canned anchovy
   fillets, drained

1 cup olive oil

1 cup coarsely chopped
   Italian parsley

⅔ cup sour cream

1 lb/450 g dried spaghetti

2 tbsp butter

salt and pepper

ripe black olives, to garnish

1 Remove any bones from the tuna, then put the tuna, anchovies, oil, and parsley into a food processor or blender and process until a smooth sauce is formed.

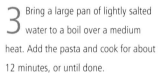

2 Spoon the sour cream into the food processor or blender and process again for a few seconds to blend thoroughly. Season to taste with salt and pepper.

3 Bring a large pan of lightly salted water to a boil over a medium heat. Add the pasta and cook for about 12 minutes, or until done.

4 Drain the pasta, return to the pan and put over a medium heat. Add the butter and toss well to coat. Spoon in the sauce and, using 2 forks, quickly toss into the pasta.

5 Remove the pan from the heat and transfer the pasta to 4 large, warmed serving plates. Garnish with the olives and serve immediately.

149

red mullet fillets with orecchiette

serves four

3¾ cups all-purpose flour

8 red mullet fillets

2 tbsp butter

⅝ cup fish bouillon

1 tbsp crushed almonds

1 tsp pink peppercorns

1 orange, peeled and cut
    into segments

1 tbsp orange liqueur

grated peel of 1 orange

1 lb/450 g dried orecchiette

1 tbsp olive oil

⅝ cup heavy cream

4 tbsp amaretto

salt and pepper

TO GARNISH

2 tbsp snipped fresh chives

1 tbsp toasted almonds

1 Season the flour with salt and pepper and sprinkle into a shallow bowl. Press the fish fillets into the flour to coat. Melt the butter in a skillet over a low heat. Add the fish and cook for about 3 minutes, or until browned.

2 Add the fish bouillon to the skillet and cook for 4 minutes. Carefully transfer the fish to a heatproof plate, cover with foil and keep warm.

3 Add the almonds, pink peppercorns, half the orange, the orange liqueur, and orange peel to the skillet. Simmer until the liquid has reduced by half.

4 Meanwhile, bring a large pan of lightly salted water to a boil over a medium heat. Add the pasta and cook for 15 minutes, or until done.

5 Meanwhile, season the sauce with salt and pepper and stir in the cream and amaretto. Cook for 2 minutes. Return the fish fillets to the skillet to coat with the sauce.

6 Drain the pasta and transfer to a serving dish. Top with the fish fillets and the sauce. Garnish with the remaining orange segments, chives, and toasted almonds. Serve.

squid & macaroni stew

serves four

2 cups dried short-cut macaroni or
 other small pasta shapes

6 tbsp olive oil

2 onions, sliced

12 oz/350 g prepared squid, cut
 into 1½-inch/4-cm strips

1 cup fish bouillon

⅝ cup red wine

12 oz/350 g tomatoes, peeled and
 sliced thinly

2 tbsp tomato paste

1 tsp dried oregano

2 bay leaves

2 tbsp chopped fresh parsley

salt and pepper

1 Bring a large pan of lightly salted water to a boil over a medium heat. Add the macaroni and cook for 3 minutes. Drain, then return to the pan. Cover and keep warm.

2 Heat the oil in a pan over a medium heat. Add the onions and cook until translucent. Add the squid and bouillon and simmer for 5 minutes. Pour in the wine and add the tomatoes, tomato paste, oregano, and bay leaves. Bring to a boil, then season to taste with salt and pepper and cook for 5 minutes.

3 Stir the macaroni into the pan, then cover and simmer for about 10 minutes, or until the squid and

macaroni are tender and the sauce has thickened. If the sauce remains too liquid, uncover the pan and continue cooking for a few minutes.

4 Remove the bay leaves and discard. Set aside a little parsley and stir the remainder into the pan. Transfer to a large, warmed serving dish and sprinkle over the remaining parsley. Serve immediately.

noodles with shrimp

serves four

8 oz/225 g fine thread egg noodles

2 tbsp peanut oil

1 garlic clove, minced

½ tsp ground star anise

1 bunch scallions, cut into
2-inch/5-cm pieces

24 raw jumbo shrimp, shelled with
tails intact

2 tbsp light soy sauce

2 tsp lime juice

lime wedges, to garnish

1 Bring a large pan of water to a boil over a medium heat. Add the noodles and blanch for 2–3 minutes.

2 Drain the noodles thoroughly, then rinse under cold water and drain again. Keep warm and set aside until required.

3 Heat a large wok over a high heat. Add the peanut oil and heat until almost smoking.

4 When the oil is hot, add the garlic and ground star anise to the wok and cook for 30 seconds.

5 Add the scallions and jumbo shrimp and cook for 2–3 minutes.

6 Stir in the light soy sauce, lime juice, and noodles, then mix well.

7 Cook the mixture in the wok for about 1 minute until thoroughly heated through and all the ingredients are thoroughly incorporated.

8 Spoon the noodle and shrimp mixture into a warmed serving dish. Transfer to 4 serving bowls, garnish with lime wedges and serve.

poached salmon with penne

serves four

4 x 10 oz/275 g fresh salmon steaks

2½ tbsp butter

¾ cup dry white wine

pinch of sea salt

8 peppercorns

1 fresh dill sprig

1 fresh tarragon sprig

1 lemon, sliced

4 cups dried penne

2 tbsp olive oil

¼ cup all-purpose flour

⅔ cup warm milk

juice and finely grated peel of
    2 lemons

2 oz/55 g arugula, chopped

salt and pepper

TO GARNISH

lemon slices

arugula

1 Put the salmon into a large, non-stick skillet. Add 2 tablespoons of the butter, wine, sea salt, peppercorns, dill, tarragon, and lemon slices. Bring to a boil over a medium heat, cover and simmer for 10 minutes.

2 Using a spatula, carefully remove the salmon. Strain and set aside the cooking liquid. Remove and discard the salmon skin and center bones, then put into a warmed dish, cover and keep warm.

3 Meanwhile, bring a large pan of lightly salted water to a boil over a medium heat. Add the pasta and cook for 12 minutes, or until done. Drain and sprinkle with the remaining oil. Put into a warmed serving dish, top with the salmon and keep warm.

4 Melt the remaining butter in a pan over a low heat and stir in the flour for 2 minutes. Stir in the milk and 7 tablespoons of the cooking liquid. Add the lemon juice and peel and cook for an additional 10 minutes.

5 Add the arugula to the sauce, stir gently and season to taste with salt and pepper.

6 Pour the sauce over the salmon, garnish with lemon slices and arugula. Serve immediately.

salmon lasagna rolls

serves four

8 sheets green lasagna

1 onion, sliced

1 tbsp butter

½ red bell pepper, chopped

1 zucchini, diced

1 tsp chopped fresh gingerroot

4½ oz/125 g exotic mushrooms, chopped coarsely

8 oz/225 g fresh salmon fillet, skinned and cut into chunks

2 tbsp dry sherry

2 tsp cornstarch

3 tbsp all-purpose flour

1½ tbsp butter

1¼ cups milk

¼ cup freshly grated cheddar cheese

¼ cup fresh white bread crumbs

salt and pepper

mixed salad greens, to serve

1 Put the lasagna sheets in a large shallow dish. Cover with plenty of boiling water. Cook in the microwave on HIGH for 5 minutes. Let stand, covered, for a few minutes before draining. Rinse in cold water and lay the sheets out on a clean counter.

2 Put the onion and butter into a bowl. Cover and cook on HIGH for 2 minutes. Add the bell pepper, zucchini, and ginger. Cover and cook on HIGH for 3 minutes.

3 Add the mushrooms and salmon to the bowl. Mix the sherry into the cornstarch, then stir into the bowl. Cover and cook on HIGH for 4 minutes, or until the fish flakes when tested with a fork. Season to taste with salt and pepper.

4 Whisk the flour, butter, and milk together in a bowl. Cook on HIGH for 3–4 minutes, whisking every minute, to give a sauce of coating consistency. Stir in half the cheese and season to taste.

5 Spoon the salmon filling in equal quantities along the shorter side of each lasagna sheet. Roll up to enclose the filling. Arrange in a lightly greased large rectangular dish. Pour over the sauce and sprinkle over the remaining cheese and bread crumbs.

6 Cook on HIGH for 3 minutes until heated through. Lightly brown under a preheated hot broiler before serving. Transfer to 4 serving plates and serve with salad greens.

ravioli of lemon sole & haddock

serves four

1 lb/450 g lemon sole
    fillets, skinned

1 lb/450 g haddock fillets, skinned

3 eggs beaten

1 lb/450 g cooked potato gnocchi

3 cups fresh bread crumbs

¼ cup heavy cream

1 lb/450 g Homemade Pasta
    Dough, made without tarragon
    (see page 24)

1¼ cups Italian Red Wine Sauce
    (see page 96)

⅔ cup freshly grated
    Parmesan cheese

salt and pepper

COOK'S TIP

When making square ravioli,
divide the dough into 2 pieces.
Wrap half in plastic wrap and
cover with a damp dish towel.
Roll out the other half thinly and
spoon in the filling at regular
intervals. Brush the spaces in
between with water. Roll out the
second sheet of dough and lift
into position. Press to seal. Cut
out with a ravioli cutter or knife.

1 Flake the lemon sole and haddock fillets with a fork and transfer the flesh to a large mixing bowl.

2 Mix the eggs, cooked potato gnocchi, bread crumbs, and cream together in a bowl until thoroughly mixed. Add the fish to the bowl containing the gnocchi and season to taste with salt and pepper.

3 Roll out the Pasta Dough (see page 24) onto a lightly floured counter and cut out 3-inch/7.5-cm circles with a plain cutter.

4 Put a spoonful of the fish filling onto each circle. Dampen the edges slightly and fold the pasta circle over, pressing together to seal.

5 Bring a large pan of lightly salted water to a boil over a medium heat. Add the ravioli and cook for 2–4 minutes, or until cooked.

6 Drain the ravioli, using a draining spoon, and transfer to a large serving dish. Pour over the Italian Red Wine Sauce (see page 96) and sprinkle with Parmesan cheese. Serve.

linguine with sardines

serves four

8 sardines, filleted

1 fennel bulb

4 tbsp olive oil

3 garlic cloves, sliced

1 tsp chili flakes

12 oz/350 g dried linguine

½ tsp finely grated lemon peel

1 tbsp lemon juice

2 tbsp pine nuts, toasted

2 tbsp chopped fresh parsley

salt and pepper

1 Wash the sardine fillets and pat dry on paper towels. Using a sharp knife, coarsely chop them into large pieces and set aside. Trim the fennel bulb, discard the outer leaves and slice very thinly.

2 Heat 2 tablespoons of the oil in large, heavy-bottomed skillet ov a medium-high heat. Add the garlic and chili flakes and cook for 1 minute then add the fennel slices. Cook, stirring occasionally, for 4–5 minutes, or until softened. Reduce the heat, ad the sardines, and cook for about 3–4 minutes, or until just cooked.

3 Meanwhile, bring a pan of lightl salted water to a boil over a medium heat. Add the pasta and cook for about 8–10 minutes, or until done Drain well and return to the pan.

4 Add the lemon peel, lemon juice pine nuts, and parsley to the sardines and toss together. Season to taste with salt and pepper. Add to the pasta with the remaining oil and toss together gently. Transfer to a warmed serving dish and serve immediately.

ermicelli with clams

serves four

4 oz/400 g dried vermicelli, spaghetti or other long pasta

 tbsp olive oil

 tbsp butter

 onions, chopped

 garlic cloves, chopped

 4 oz/400 g canned clams in brine

 cup white wine

 tbsp chopped fresh parsley

 tsp dried oregano

epper

inch of freshly grated nutmeg

O GARNISH

 tbsp Parmesan cheese shavings

resh basil sprigs

1 Bring a large pan of lightly salted water to a boil over a medium heat. Add the pasta and cook until done. Drain the pasta thoroughly, return to the pan and add the butter. Cover, shake well and keep warm.

2 Heat the oil and the butter in a pan over a medium heat. Add the onions and cook until translucent. Stir in the garlic and cook for 1 minute.

3 Strain the liquid from the canned clams into bowl. Add half of the liquid to the pan with the white wine and discard the remaining liquid. Stir, then bring to simmering point and simmer for 3 minutes.

4 Add the clams, parsley, and oregano to the pan and season with pepper and nutmeg. Reduce the heat and cook until heated through.

5 Transfer the pasta to a warmed serving dish and pour over the sauce. Garnish with Parmesan cheese and basil sprigs. Serve immediately.

corsican clam spaghetti

serves four

14 oz/400 g dried spaghetti

salt and pepper

CORSICAN CLAM SAUCE

2 lb/900 g live clams

4 tbsp olive oil

3 large garlic cloves, minced

pinch of chili flakes (optional)

2 lb/900 g tomatoes, peeled and
chopped, with juice set aside

½ cup pitted green or ripe black
olives, chopped

1 tbsp chopped fresh oregano or
½ tsp dried oregano

1 To make the sauce, put the clams
into a bowl of lightly salted water
and let soak for 30 minutes. Rinse
them under cold running water and
scrub lightly to remove any sand from
the shells.

2 Discard any broken clams or open
clams that refuse to close when
firmly tapped. This indicates they are
dead and can cause food poisoning if
eaten. Put the clams soak into a large
bowl of water and let soak. Meanwhile,
bring a large pan of lightly salted water
to a boil over a medium heat.

3 Heat the oil in a large skillet over
a medium heat. Add the garlic
and chili flakes (if using), and cook,
stirring constantly, for about 2 minutes.

4 Stir in the tomatoes, olives, and
oregano. Reduce the heat and
simmer, stirring frequently, until the
tomatoes soften and start to break up.
Cover and simmer for 10 minutes.

5 Meanwhile, add the pasta to the
pan of boiling water, bring back
to a boil, and cook for 8–10 minutes,
or until done. Drain the pasta

thoroughly, and set aside about ½ cu
of the cooking liquid. Return the pas
to the pan and keep warm.

6 Add the clams and reserved
cooking liquid to the sauce and
stir. Bring to a boil over a medium
heat, stirring constantly. Discard any
clams that have not opened and
transfer the sauce to a larger pan.

7 Add the pasta to the sauce and
toss until well coated, then
transfer the pasta to 4 large, warmed
serving dishes. Serve immediately.

pasta with broccoli & anchovy sauce

serves four

1 lb/500 g 2 oz broccoli

14 oz/400 g dried orecchiette

5 tbsp olive oil

2 large garlic cloves, minced

1¾ oz/50 g canned anchovy fillets
   in oil, drained, and
   chopped finely

2 oz/55 g fresh Parmesan cheese

2 oz/55 g fresh romano cheese

salt and pepper

1 Bring 2 pans of lightly salted water to a boil over a medium heat. Chop the broccoli flowerets and stems into small, bite-size pieces. Add the broccoli to 1 pan and cook until very tender. Drain and set aside.

2 Put the pasta into the other pan of boiling water and cook for 10–12 minutes, or until done.

3 Meanwhile, heat the oil in a large pan over a medium heat. Add the garlic and cook for 3 minutes, stirring constantly, without letting it brown. Add the chopped anchovies and cook for about 3 minutes, stirring and mashing with a wooden spoon to break them up. Finely grate the Parmesan and romano cheeses on separate plates.

4 Drain the pasta thoroughly, add to the pan of anchovies and stir. Add the broccoli and stir to mix.

5 Add the grated Parmesan and romano cheeses to the pasta and stir constantly over a medium–high heat until the cheeses melt and the pasta and broccoli are coated.

6 Adjust the seasoning to taste— the anchovies and cheeses are salty, so you will only need to add pepper. Transfer to 4 warmed bowls and serve immediately.

pan-cooked shrimp

serves four

4 garlic cloves

20–24 large, raw
   shrimp, unshelled

8 tbsp butter

4 tbsp olive oil

6 tbsp brandy

2 tbsp chopped fresh parsley

salt and pepper

12 oz/350 g freshly cooked pasta,
   to serve

1 Using a sharp knife, peel and
slice the garlic.

2 Wash the shrimp and pat dry on
paper towels.

3 Melt the butter with the oil in a
large skillet over a high heat. Add
the garlic and shrimp, and cook,
stirring constantly, for 3–4 minutes, or
until the shrimp turn pink.

4 Sprinkle with brandy and season
to taste with salt and pepper and
sprinkle with chopped parsley. Serve
immediately with freshly cooked pasta.

spaghetti al vongole

serves four

2 lb/900 g live clams, scrubbed

2 tbsp olive oil

1 large onion, chopped finely

2 garlic cloves, chopped finely

1 tsp fresh thyme leaves

²⁄₃ cup white wine

14 oz/400 g canned
  chopped tomatoes

12 oz/350 g dried spaghetti

1 tbsp chopped fresh parsley

salt and pepper

4 fresh thyme sprigs, to garnish

COOK'S TIP

If you are able to get only very
large clams, set a few aside in
their shells to garnish and
shell the rest.

1 Soak the clams in salted water for 30 minutes. Rinse in cold water and scrub lightly. Discard any broken or open clams and put into a pan with just the water clinging to their shells. Cook, covered, over a high heat for 3–4 minutes until opened. Remove from the heat, strain and set aside any liquid. Discard any that remain closed.

2 Heat the oil in a pan over a low heat. Add the onion and cook for 10 minutes, or until softened, but not colored. Add the garlic and thyme, and cook for an additional 30 seconds.

3 Increase the heat and add the white wine. Simmer rapidly unti reduced and syrupy. Add the tomatoe and reserved clam liquid. Cover and simmer for 15 minutes. Uncover and simmer for an additional 15 minutes, or until thickened. Season to taste wi salt and pepper.

4 Meanwhile, bring a large pan o lightly salted water to a boil ove a medium heat. Add the pasta and cook for 8–10 minutes, or until done Drain the pasta thoroughly and retur to the pan.

5 Add the clams to the tomato sauce and heat through for 2–3 minutes. Add the parsley and sti then add the tomato sauce and mix. Transfer to 4 warmed serving bowls and garnish with thyme sprigs. Serve

farfalle with a medley of seafood

serves four

12 raw tiger shrimp

12 raw shrimp

1 lb/450 g fillet of red snapper

4 tbsp butter

12 scallops, shelled

4½ oz/125 g freshwater shrimp

juice and finely grated peel of
    1 lemon

pinch of saffron powder or threads

4 cups vegetable bouillon

⅝ cup rose petal vinegar
    (see page 109)

1 lb/450 g dried farfalle

1 tbsp olive oil

⅝ cup white wine

1 tbsp pink peppercorns

4 oz/115 g baby carrots

⅝ cup heavy cream

salt and pepper

1 fresh Italian parsley sprig,
    to garnish

1 Shell and devein the shrimp. Thinly slice the red snapper. Melt the butter in a pan over a low heat. Add the seafood and cook for about 1–2 minutes.

2 Season with pepper. Add the lemon juice and grated peel. Very carefully add a pinch of saffron powder or a few strands of saffron to the cooking juices (not to the seafood).

3 Remove the seafood from the pan. Set aside and keep warm.

4 Return the pan to the heat and add the vegetable bouillon. Bring to a boil and reduce by one third. Add the rose-petal vinegar and cook for 4 minutes, or until reduced.

5 Bring a large pan of lightly salted water to a boil over a medium heat. Add the pasta and oil and cook until done. Drain the pasta thoroughly, then transfer to a large serving plate and top with the seafood.

6 Add the wine, peppercorns, and carrots to the pan and reduce the sauce for 6 minutes. Add the cream and simmer for 2 minutes.

7 Pour the sauce over the seafood and pasta and garnish with a parsley sprig. Serve immediately.

farfallini buttered lobster

serves four

2 x 1 lb 9 oz/700 g lobsters, split
　into halves
juice and grated peel of 1 lemon
½ cup butter
4 tbsp fresh white bread crumbs
2 tbsp brandy
5 tbsp heavy cream
1 lb/450 g dried farfallini
⅔ cup freshly grated
　Parmesan cheese
salt and pepper
TO GARNISH
1 kiwi fruit, sliced
4 cooked, unshelled jumbo shrimp
fresh dill sprigs

1 Carefully discard the stomach sac, vein, and gills from each lobster. Remove all the meat from the tail and chop. Crack the legs, remove the meat and chop. Transfer the meat to a large bowl and add the lemon juice and grated lemon peel.

2 Clean the shells thoroughly and put into a warm oven at 325°F/160°C to dry out.

3 Melt 2 tablespoons of the butter in a skillet over a low heat. Add the bread crumbs and cook for about 3 minutes, or until crisp and golden.

4 Melt the remaining butter in a pan over a low heat. Add the lobster meat and heat through gently. Add the brandy and cook for an additional 3 minutes, then add the cream, and season to taste with salt and pepper.

5 Meanwhile, bring a large pan of lightly salted water to a boil over a medium heat. Add the pasta and cook for about 12 minutes, or until done. Drain the pasta thoroughly and spoon the pasta into the clean shells. Top with the buttered lobster and sprinkle with a little grated Parmesan cheese and the bread crumbs. Cook under a preheated hot broiler for 2–3 minutes, or until golden brown.

6 Transfer the lobster shells to a large, warmed serving dish. Garnish with kiwi fruit, jumbo shrimp, and dill sprigs, then serve immediately.

thai noodles

serves four

12 oz/350 g cooked, shelled
   jumbo shrimp
4 oz/115 g flat rice noodles or
   rice vermicelli
4 tbsp vegetable oil
2 garlic cloves, chopped finely
1 egg
2 tbsp lemon juice
4½ tsp Thai fish sauce
½ tsp sugar
2 tbsp roasted peanuts, chopped
½ tsp cayenne pepper
2 scallions, cut into
   1-inch/2.5-cm pieces
1 cup fresh bean sprouts
1 tbsp chopped fresh cilantro

1 Drain the jumbo shrimp on paper towels to remove any excess moisture. Set aside. Cook the rice noodles according to the package instructions. Drain thoroughly and set aside until required.

2 Heat a large wok over a high heat. Add the oil and when hot, add the garlic. Cook, stirring constantly, until just golden. Add the egg and stir quickly to break it up. Cook for a few seconds.

3 Add the shrimp and noodles, scraping down the sides of the wok to ensure they mix with the egg and garlic.

4 Add the lemon juice, fish sauce, sugar, half the peanuts, the cayenne, scallions, and half the bean sprouts stirring quickly all the time. Cook for an additional 2 minutes.

5 Transfer to a large, warmed serving plate. Top with the remaining peanuts and bean sprouts, and sprinkle with the chopped cilantro. Serve immediately.

sesame noodles with shrimp

serves four

1 garlic clove, chopped

1 scallion, chopped

1 small fresh red chile, seeded
  and sliced

1 tbsp chopped fresh cilantro

10½ oz/300 g fine egg noodles

2 tbsp vegetable oil

2 tsp sesame oil

1 tsp shrimp paste

2 cups raw shrimp, shelled

2 tbsp lime juice

2 tbsp Thai fish sauce

1 tsp sesame seeds, toasted

1 Put the garlic, onion, chile, and cilantro into a mortar and pound with a pestle to a smooth paste.

2 Bring a large pan of water to a boil over a medium heat. Add the noodles and cook for 4 minutes, or according to the package instructions.

3 Heat a large wok over a medium heat. Add the vegetable and sesame oils and when hot, stir in the shrimp paste and ground cilantro mixture. Stir for about 1 minute.

4 Stir in the shrimp and cook for 2 minutes. Stir in the lime juice and fish sauce and cook for 1 minute.

5 Drain the noodles and toss them into the wok. Transfer to 4 large serving bowls, sprinkle with the sesame seeds and serve immediately.

spaghetti & shellfish

2 cups dried spaghetti, broken into
   15-cm/6-inch lengths

2 tbsp olive oil

1¼ cups chicken bouillon

1 tsp lemon juice

1 small cauliflower, cut
   into flowerets

2 carrots, sliced thinly

4 oz/115 g snow peas

4 tbsp butter

1 onion, sliced

8 oz/225 g zucchini, sliced

1 garlic clove, chopped

12 oz/350 g frozen, cooked, shelled
   shrimp, thawed

2 tbsp chopped fresh parsley

¼ cup freshly grated
   Parmesan cheese

½ tsp paprika

salt and pepper

4 unshelled, cooked shrimp,
   to garnish

crusty bread, to serve

1 Bring a pan of lightly salted water to a boil over a medium heat. Add the pasta and and cook until done. Drain the pasta thoroughly and return to the pan. Toss with the oil, cover and keep warm.

2 Bring the chicken bouillon and lemon juice to a boil over a medium heat. Add the cauliflower and carrots and cook for 3–4 minutes. Remove from the pan and set aside. Add the snow peas to the pan and cook for 1–2 minutes. Set aside with the other vegetables.

3 Melt half the butter in a large skillet over a medium heat. Add the onion and zucchini and cook for about 3 minutes. Add the garlic and shrimp and cook for an additional 2–3 minutes, or until heated through.

4 Stir in the reserved vegetables and heat through. Season to taste with salt and pepper and stir in the remaining butter.

5 Transfer the pasta to a warmed serving dish. Pour over the sauce and add the parsley. Toss well until coated. Sprinkle over the Parmesan cheese and paprika and garnish with the shrimp. Serve with crusty bread.

sicilian pasta

serves four

6 tbsp olive oil

1 cup fresh white bread crumbs

1 lb/450 g broccoli, cut into
   small flowerets

12 oz/350 g dried tagliatelle

4 canned anchovy fillets, drained
   and chopped

2 garlic cloves, sliced

grated peel of 1 lemon

large pinch of chili flakes

salt and pepper

freshly grated Parmesan cheese,
   to serve

1 Heat 2 tablespoons of the oil in a
skillet over a medium heat. Add
the bread crumbs and cook for
4–5 minutes, or until golden and crisp.
Drain thoroughly on paper towels.

2 Bring a large pan of lightly salted
water to a boil over a medium
heat. Add the broccoli and blanch for
3 minutes, then drain, and set aside
the water. Refresh the broccoli under
cold water and drain again. Pat dry on
paper towels and set aside.

3 Bring the water back to a boil and
add the pasta and cook for
8–10 minutes, or until done.

4 Meanwhile, heat 2 tablespoons
of the remaining oil in a large,
heavy-bottomed skillet over a low
heat. Add the anchovies and cook for
about 1 minute, then mash with a
wooden spoon to a paste. Add the
garlic, lemon peel, and chili flakes.
Cook for 2 minutes, then add the
broccoli and cook for 3–4 minutes, or
until heated through.

5 Drain the cooked pasta and
add to the broccoli mixture with
the remaining oil. Season to taste with
salt and pepper. Toss together well.

6 Transfer the pasta to 4 warmed
serving plates. Top with the
cooked bread crumbs and Parmesan
cheese, and serve immediately.

pasta puttanesca

serves four

3 tbsp extra virgin olive oil

1 large red onion, chopped finely

4 canned anchovy fillets, drained

pinch of chili flakes

2 garlic cloves, chopped finely

14 oz/400 g canned
    chopped tomatoes

2 tbsp tomato paste

8 oz/225 g dried spaghetti

¼ cup pitted ripe black olives,
    chopped coarsely

¼ cup pitted green olives,
    chopped coarsely

1 tbsp capers, rinsed and drained

4 sun-dried tomatoes in oil, drained
    and chopped coarsely

salt and pepper

fresh herb sprigs, to garnish

2 Meanwhile, bring a pan of lightly salted water to a boil over a medium heat. Add the pasta and cook for about 8–10 minutes, or until done.

3 Add the olives, capers, and sun-dried tomatoes to the sauce. Simmer for an additional 2–3 minutes. Season to taste with salt and pepper.

4 Drain the pasta thoroughly and stir in the sauce. Toss thoroughly to mix. Transfer to a large, warmed serving dish and garnish with herb sprigs. Serve immediately.

1 Heat the oil in a skillet over a low heat. Add the onion, anchovies, and chili flakes and cook for about 0 minutes, or until softened. Add the garlic and cook for 30 seconds. Stir in the tomatoes and tomato paste and ring to a boil. Simmer for 10 minutes.

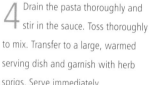

saffron mussel tagliatelle

serves four

2 lb 4 oz/1 kg mussels

⅔ cup white wine

1 medium onion, chopped finely

2 tbsp butter

2 garlic cloves, minced

2 tsp cornstarch

1 cup heavy cream

pinch of saffron threads or
saffron powder

1 egg yolk

juice of ½ lemon

1 lb/450 g dried tagliatelle

salt and pepper

3 tbsp chopped fresh parsley,
to garnish

1 Pull the "beards" off the mussels and scrub in cold water. Discard any that refuse to open when sharply tapped. Put the wine and onion into a large pan and bring to a boil over a high heat. Add the mussels, cover and cook, shaking the pan, for 4–6 minutes, or until the shells open.

2 Drain and set aside the cooking liquid. Discard any mussels that remain closed. Set aside a few mussels for the garnish and remove the remainder from their shells.

3 Strain the cooking liquid into a pan. Bring to a boil over a medium heat and reduce by about half. Remove the pan from the heat.

4 Melt the butter in a pan over a low heat. Add the garlic and cook, stirring frequently, for 2 minutes, until golden. Stir in the cornstarch and cook, stirring, for 1 minute. Gradually stir in the cooking liquid and the cream. Crush the saffron threads and add to the pan. Season to taste with salt and pepper and simmer for 2–3 minutes, or until thickened.

5 Stir in the egg yolk, lemon juice, and shelled mussels. Do not let the mixture boil.

6 Meanwhile, bring a pan of lightly salted water to a boil over a medium heat. Add the pasta and cook until done. Drain and transfer to a serving dish. Add the mussel sauce and toss. Garnish with the parsley and reserved mussels, then serve.

pasta shells with mussels

serves four to six

2 lb 12 oz/1.25 kg mussels

1 cup dry white wine

2 large onions, chopped

8 tbsp unsalted butter

6 large garlic cloves, chopped finely

5 tbsp chopped fresh parsley

1 cup heavy cream

3½ cups dried pasta shells

1 tsp olive oil

salt and pepper

crusty bread, to serve

1 Pull the "beards" off the mussels and scrub in cold water. Discard any that refuse to close when sharply tapped. Put the wine and 1 of the onions into a large pan and bring to a boil over a high heat. Add the mussels, cover and cook, shaking the pan frequently, for 4–6 minutes, or until the shells open.

2 Remove the pan from the heat. Drain the mussels and set aside the cooking liquid. Discard any mussels that remain closed. Strain the cooking liquid through a clean dish towel into a glass pitcher or bowl and set aside.

3 Melt the butter in a pan over a medium heat. Add the remaining onion and cook until translucent. Stir in the garlic and cook for 1 minute. Gradually stir in the reserved cooking liquid. Stir in the parsley and cream. Season to taste with salt and pepper, then bring to simmering point over a low heat.

COOK'S TIP

Pasta shells are ideal because the sauce collects in the cavities and impregnates the pasta with flavor.

4 Meanwhile, bring a large pan of lightly salted water to a boil over a medium heat. Add the pasta and oil and cook until done. Drain the pasta thoroughly, return to the pan, cover, and keep warm.

5 Set aside a few mussels for the garnish and remove the remainder from their shells. Stir the shelled mussels into the cream sauce and warm briefly.

6 Transfer the pasta to a large, warmed serving dish. Pour over the sauce and toss well to coat. Garnish with the reserved mussels and serve immediately with crusty bread.

spaghettini with crab

serves four

1 dressed crab, about 1 lb/450 g
  including the shell
12 oz/350 g dried spaghettini
6 tbsp extra virgin olive oil
1 fresh red chile, seeded and
  chopped finely
2 garlic cloves, chopped finely
3 tbsp chopped fresh parsley
2 tbsp lemon juice
1 tsp finely grated lemon peel
salt and pepper
lemon wedges, to garnish

COOK'S TIP
If you prefer to buy your
own fresh crab you will need a
large crab weighing about
2 lb 4 oz/1 kg.

1 Using a knife, scoop the meat
from the crab shell into a bowl.
Mix the white and brown meat lightly
together and set aside.

2 Bring a large pan of lightly salted
water to a boil over a medium
heat. Add the pasta and cook for about
8–10 minutes, or until done. Drain
thoroughly and return to the pan.

3 Meanwhile, heat 2 tablespoons
of the oil in a skillet over a low
heat. Add the chile and garlic and cook
for 30 seconds, then add the crab
meat, chopped parsley, lemon juice,
and lemon peel. Cook for an additional
minute, or until the crab meat is just
heated through.

4 Add the crab mixture to the pasta
with the remaining oil and season
to taste with salt and pepper. Toss
together thoroughly, then transfer to
a large, warmed serving dish. Garnish
with a few lemon wedges and
serve immediately.

neapolitan salad

serves four

1 lb/450 g prepared squid, cut
  into strips

1 lb 10 oz/750 g cooked mussels

1 lb/450 g cooked cockles in
  brine, drained

⅝ cup white wine

1¼ cups olive oil

2 cups dried campanelle or other
  small pasta shapes

juice of 1 lemon

1 bunch fresh chives, snipped

1 bunch fresh parsley,
  chopped finely

4 large tomatoes

mixed salad greens

salt and pepper

1 fresh basil sprig, to garnish

1 Put all the seafood into a large
bowl. Pour over the wine and half
the oil, then set aside for 6 hours.

2 Put the seafood mixture into a
pan and simmer over a low heat
for 10 minutes. Let cool.

3 Bring a large pan of lightly salted
water to a boil over a medium
heat. Add the pasta and cook for about
8–10 minutes, or until done. Drain
thoroughly and refresh in cold water.

4 Strain off about half of the
cooking liquid from the seafood
and discard the rest. Mix in the lemon
juice, chives, chopped parsley, and the
remaining oil. Season to taste with salt
and pepper. Drain the pasta and add to
the seafood.

5 Cut the tomatoes into fourths.
Shred the salad greens and arrange
them at the bottom of a large salad
bowl. Spoon in the seafood salad and
garnish with the tomato fourths and a
fresh basil sprig, then serve.

VARIATION

You can substitute cooked
scallops for the mussels and
clams in brine for the cockles.

pasta vongole

serves four

1 lb 8 oz/675 g live clams or
  10 oz/280 g canned
  clams, drained

2 tbsp olive oil

2 garlic cloves, chopped finely

14 oz/400 g mixed raw seafood,
  such as shrimp and squid

⅔ cup white wine

⅔ cup fish bouillon

1 lb 8 oz/675 g fresh pasta or
  12 oz/350 g dried pasta

2 tbsp chopped fresh tarragon

salt and pepper

VARIATION

Red clam sauce can be made by
adding 8 tbsp of tomato paste
to the sauce along with the
bouillon in step 4. Follow
the same cooking method.

1 If you are using live clams, scrub
  them clean and discard any that
  re already open.

2 Heat the oil in a large skillet over
  a medium heat. Add the garlic
and the clams and cook for 2 minutes,
shaking the skillet to ensure that all of
the clams are coated in the oil.

3 Add the remaining seafood
  mixture to the skillet and cook for
an additional 2 minutes.

4 Pour the wine and bouillon over
  the mixed seafood and garlic.
Bring to a boil over a medium heat,
then cover the pan, reduce the heat
and simmer for 8–10 minutes, or until
the shells open. Discard any clams or
mussels that remain closed.

5 Meanwhile, bring a large pan of
  lightly salted water to a boil over
a medium heat. Add the pasta and
cook until done. Drain thoroughly.

6 Stir the chopped tarragon into the
  sauce and season to taste with
salt and pepper.

7 Transfer the pasta to 4 large,
  warmed serving plates and pour
over the sauce. Serve immediately.

singapore noodles

8 oz/225 g dried egg noodles

6 tbsp vegetable oil

4 eggs, beaten

3 garlic cloves, minced

1½ tsp chili powder

8 oz/225 g skinless, boneless
    chicken, cut into thin strips

3 celery stalks, sliced

1 green bell pepper, seeded
    and sliced

4 scallions, sliced

1 oz/25 g water chestnuts, cut
    into fourths

2 fresh red chiles, sliced

2½ cups cooked, shelled shrimp

3 cups bean sprouts

2 tsp sesame oil

COOK'S TIP

When mixing precooked
ingredients into the dish, such as
the egg and noodles, ensure that
they are heated right through
and are hot when ready to serve.

1 Soak the noodles in boiling water for 4 minutes or until soft. Set aside to drain on paper towels.

2 Heat a wok over a high heat. Add 2 tablespoons of the oil and when hot, add the eggs and stir until set. Remove the cooked eggs from the wok, set aside, and keep warm.

3 Add the remaining oil to the wok. Add the garlic and chili powder, and cook for 30 seconds.

4 Add the chicken strips and cook for about 4–5 minutes, or until starting to brown.

5 Stir in the celery, green bell pepper, scallions, water chestnuts, and chiles and cook for an additional 8 minutes, or until the chicken is cooked through.

6 Add the shrimp and the reserved noodles to the wok, together with the bean sprouts, and toss to mix well.

7 Break the cooked egg with a fork and sprinkle it over the noodles, then sprinkle the sesame oil over the noodles. Serve immediately.

Vegetable Pasta

The pasta and rice recipes in this chapter offer something special for every occasion: filling vegetarian meals, unusual vegetable side dishes, and main courses. You could even take many of the salads on a picnic and, of course, they are perfect as accompaniments for summer barbecues. Some are classic dishes, such as Traditional Cannelloni, Pesto Pasta, and Spaghetti with Peas & Cream. Others are imaginative and sometimes surprising new combinations of vegetables and pasta. Try Artichoke & Olive Pasta, Spinach & Exotic Mushroom Lasagna, Vegetable Ravioli, and Three-Cheese Macaroni for a family meal, or Fried Vegetable Noodles as a side dish.

pasta with nuts & cheese

serves four

1 cup pine nuts

3 cups dried pasta shapes

1¼ cups broccoli flowerets

2 zucchini, sliced

1 cup full-fat soft cheese

⅔ cup milk

1 tbsp chopped fresh basil

4½ oz/125 g white
    mushrooms, sliced

3 oz/85 g blue cheese, crumbled

salt and pepper

fresh basil sprigs, to garnish

salad greens, to serve

1 Sprinkle the pine nuts onto a cookie sheet and cook under a preheated broiler, turning occasionally, until lightly browned. Set aside.

2 Bring a large pan of lightly salted water to a boil over a medium heat. Add the pasta and cook for about 8–10 minutes, or until done.

3 Bring a large pan of lightly salted water to a boil over a medium heat. Add the broccoli and zucchini and cook for 5 minutes.

4 Put the soft cheese into a pan and heat over a low heat, stirring. Stir in the milk. Add the basil and mushrooms, and cook for 2–3 minutes. Stir in the blue cheese and season to taste with salt and pepper.

5 Drain the pasta and vegetables, and mix together. Pour the cheese and mushroom sauce over, and add the pine nuts. Toss gently to mix them in. Transfer to 4 serving dishes and garnish with basil sprig. Serve with salad greens.

patriotic pasta

serves four

4 cups dried farfalle

1 lb/450 g cherry tomatoes

3 oz/85 g arugula

4 tbsp olive oil

salt and pepper

fresh romano cheese, to garnish

1 Bring a large pan of lightly salted water to a boil over a medium heat. Add the pasta and cook until done. Drain the pasta thoroughly and return to the pan.

2 Cut the cherry tomatoes in half and trim the arugula.

3 Heat the oil in a large pan. over a medium heat. Add the tomatoes and cook for 1 minute. Add the pasta and the arugula, and stir gently to mix. Heat through and season to taste with salt and pepper.

4 Meanwhile, using a vegetable peeler, shave thin slices of romano cheese.

5 Transfer the pasta and vegetables to a large, warmed serving dish. Garnish with the romano cheese shavings and serve immediately.

COOK'S TIP

Romano cheese is a hard sheep's milk cheese that resembles Parmesan and is often used for grating over a variety of dishes. It has a sharp flavor and is only used in small quantities.

tagliatelle & garlic sauce

serves four

2 tbsp walnut oil

1 bunch scallions, sliced

2 garlic cloves, sliced thinly

8 oz/225 g mushrooms, sliced

500 g/1 lb 2 oz fresh green and
white tagliatelle

1¼ cups frozen chopped leaf
spinach, thawed, and drained

4½ oz/125 g full-fat soft cheese
flavored with garlic and herbs

4 tbsp light cream

4 tbsp chopped, unsalted
pistachio nuts

2 tbsp shredded fresh basil

salt and pepper

4 fresh basil sprigs, to garnish

Italian bread, to serve

1 Heat the walnut oil in a skillet over a low heat. Add the scallions nd garlic and cook for 1 minute, or ntil just soft. Add the mushrooms to he skillet, stir well, cover, and cook ently for 5 minutes, or until soft.

2 Meanwhile, bring a large pan of lightly salted water to a boil over medium heat. Add the pasta and cook for 3–5 minutes, or until done. Drain the pasta thoroughly and return to the pan.

3 Add the spinach to the mushrooms and heat through for 1–2 minutes. Add the cheese and let melt slightly. Stir in the cream and continue to heat without letting it boil.

4 Pour the vegetable mixture over the pasta, season to taste with salt and pepper, and mix well. Heat gently, stirring constantly, for about 2–3 minutes.

5 Transfer the pasta into a warmed serving bowl and sprinkle over the pistachio nuts and shredded basil. Garnish with fresh basil sprigs and serve with Italian bread.

pasta & chili tomatoes

serves four

10 oz/280 g dried pappardelle

3 tbsp groundnut oil

2 garlic cloves, minced

2 shallots, sliced

8 oz/225 g green beans, sliced

3½ oz/100 g cherry
  tomatoes, halved

1 tsp chili flakes

4 tbsp crunchy peanut butter

⅔ cup coconut milk

1 tbsp tomato paste

VARIATION

Add slices of chicken or beef to
the recipe and stir-fry with the
beans and pasta in step 3 for a
more substantial main meal.

1 Bring a large pan of lightly salted water to a boil over a medium heat. Add the pasta and cook for about 8–10 minutes, or until done. Drain the pasta thoroughly and set aside.

2 Meanwhile, heat a large wok over a high heat. Add the oil and when hot, add the garlic and shallots. Cook for 1 minute.

3 Add the green beans and drained pasta to the wok, and cook for about 5 minutes. Add the cherry tomatoes and mix well.

4 Mix the chili flakes, peanut butter, coconut milk, and tomato paste together. Pour the chili mixture into the wok, toss well and heat through.

5 Transfer the pasta to 4 large, warmed serving dishes and serve immediately.

vegetable ravioli

serves four

1 lb/450 g Homemade Pasta Dough
   made without tarragon
   (see page 24)

6 tbsp butter

⅔ cup light cream

¾ cup freshly grated
   Parmesan cheese

fresh basil sprigs, to garnish

FILLING

2 large eggplants

3 large zucchini

6 large tomatoes

1 large green bell pepper

1 large red bell pepper

3 garlic cloves

1 large onion

½ cup olive oil

2 tbsp tomato paste

½ tsp chopped fresh basil

salt and pepper

1 To make the filling, cut the eggplants and zucchini into 1-inch/2.5-cm chunks. Put the eggplant pieces into a strainer, sprinkle liberally with salt and set aside for 20 minutes. Rinse and drain, then pat dry on paper towels.

2 Blanch the tomatoes in boiling water for 2 minutes. Drain, peel, and chop the flesh. Core and seed the peppers and cut into 1-inch/2.5-cm dice. Chop the garlic and onion.

3 Heat the oil in a pan over a low heat. Add the garlic and onion and cook, stirring occasionally, for about 3 minutes.

4 Stir in the eggplants, zucchini, tomatoes, bell peppers, tomato paste, and basil. Season to taste with salt and pepper, cover and simmer for 20 minutes, stirring frequently.

5 Roll out the Pasta Dough (see page 24) and cut out 3-inch/7.5-cm circles with a plain cutter. Put a spoonful of the vegetable filling on each circle. Dampen the edges slightly and fold the pasta circles over, pressing together to seal.

6 Bring a pan of lightly salted water to a boil over a medium heat. Add the ravioli and cook for about 3–4 minutes. Drain and transfer to an ovenproof dish, dotting each layer with butter. Pour over the cream and sprinkle over Parmesan cheese. Cook in a preheated oven at 400°F/200°C, for 20 minutes. Garnish with a basil sprig and serve immediately.

summertime tagliatelle

serves four

1 lb 7 oz/650 g zucchini

6 tbsp olive oil

3 garlic cloves, minced

3 tbsp chopped fresh basil

2 fresh red chiles, seeded and sliced

juice of 1 large lemon

5 tbsp light cream

4 tbsp freshly grated
  Parmesan cheese

8 oz/225 g dried tagliatelle

salt and pepper

COOK'S TIP

Lime juice could be used instead
of the lemon. As limes are
usually smaller, squeeze the juice
from 2 fruits.

1 Using a swivel vegetable peeler, slice the zucchini into thin ribbons.

2 Heat the oil in a skillet over a low heat. Add the garlic and cook for 30 seconds.

3 Add the zucchini ribbons and cook, stirring constantly, for 3–5 minutes. Stir in the basil, chiles, lemon juice, cream, and Parmesan cheese and season to taste with salt and pepper. Keep warm.

4 Meanwhile, bring a large pan of lightly salted water to a boil over a medium heat. Add the pasta and cook for 8–10 minutes, or until done. Drain the pasta thoroughly and transf to a large, warmed serving bowl.

5 Pile the zucchini mixture on top the pasta and serve immediately

artichoke & olive spaghetti

serves four

2 tbsp olive oil

1 large red onion, chopped

2 garlic cloves, minced

1 tbsp lemon juice

4 baby eggplants, cut into fourths

2½ cups strained tomatoes

2 tsp superfine sugar

2 tbsp tomato paste

14 oz/400 g canned artichoke
   hearts, drained and halved

1 cup pitted ripe black olives

12 oz/350 g whole-wheat
   dried spaghetti

salt and pepper

fresh basil sprigs, to garnish

1 Heat 1 tablespoon of the oil in a large skillet over a low heat. Add the onion, garlic, lemon juice, and eggplants and cook for 4–5 minutes, or until lightly browned.

2 Pour in the strained tomatoes, season to taste with salt and pepper, and stir in the sugar and tomato paste. Bring to a boil, reduce the heat and simmer for 20 minutes.

3 Gently stir in the artichoke hearts and olives and cook for 5 minutes.

4 Meanwhile, bring a large pan of lightly salted water to a boil over a medium heat. Add the pasta and cook for 8–10 minutes, or until done. Drain the pasta thoroughly, toss in the remaining oil, and season to taste.

5 Transfer the pasta to 4 large, warmed serving bowls and top with the vegetable sauce. Garnish with basil sprigs and serve immediately.

beet cannolicchi

serves four

10½ oz/300 g dried ditalini rigati

4 tbsp olive oil

2 garlic cloves, chopped

14 oz/400 g canned
    chopped tomatoes

14 oz/400 g cooked beet, diced

2 tbsp chopped fresh basil leaves

1 tsp mustard seeds

salt and pepper

TO SERVE

mixed salad greens, tossed in
    olive oil

4 Italian plum tomatoes, sliced

1 Bring a large pan of lightly salted water to a boil over a medium heat. Add the pasta and cook for about 10 minutes, or until done. Drain the pasta thoroughly and set aside.

2 Heat the oil in a large pan over a low heat. Add the garlic and cook for 3 minutes. Add the chopped tomatoes and cook for 10 minutes.

3 Remove the pan from the heat and carefully add the beet, basil, mustard seeds, and pasta, and season to taste with salt and pepper.

4 Serve on a bed of mixed salad greens tossed in oil, and sliced plum tomatoes.

chile & red bell pepper pasta

serves four

2 red bell peppers, halved
and seeded

1 small fresh red chile

2 garlic cloves

4 tomatoes, halved

1¾ oz/50 g ground almonds

7 tbsp olive oil

1 lb 8 oz/675 g fresh pasta or
12 oz/350 g dried pasta

fresh oregano leaves, to garnish

1 Put the bell peppers, skin-side up, onto a cookie sheet with the chile, garlic, and tomatoes. Cook under a preheated hot broiler for 15 minutes, or until charred. After 10 minutes, turn the tomatoes skin-side down.

2 Put the bell peppers and chile into a plastic bag and let them sweat for 10 minutes.

3 Using a sharp knife, remove the skin from the bell peppers and chile and slice the flesh into strips.

4 Peel the garlic and peel and seed the tomatoes.

5 Put the almonds onto a cookie sheet and cook under the broiler for 2–3 minutes, or until golden.

VARIATION

Add 2 tbsp of red wine vinegar to the sauce and use as a dressing for a cold pasta salad, if you prefer.

6 Put the bell pepper, chile, garlic, and tomatoes into a food processor or blender and blend to a paste. Keep the motor running and slowly add the oil to form a thick sauce. Alternatively, put the mixture into a bowl and mash with a fork. Beat in the oil, drop by drop.

7 Stir the toasted ground almonds into the mixture.

8 Put the sauce into a pan and warm until it is heated through.

9 Bring a large pan of lightly salted water to a boil over a medium heat. Add the pasta and cook for about 8–10 minutes, or until done. Drain the pasta thoroughly and transfer to 4 large, warmed serving dishes. Pour over the sauce and toss to mix. Garnish with fresh oregano leaves and serve.

pesto pasta

serves four

3¼ cups sliced crimini mushrooms

⅔ cup vegetable bouillon

6 oz/175 g asparagus, trimmed and
cut into 2-inch/5-cm lengths

10½ oz/300 g fresh green and
white tagliatelle

14 oz/400 g canned artichoke
hearts, drained and halved

grissini, to serve

PESTO

2 large garlic cloves, minced

½ cup fresh basil leaves

6 tbsp low-fat plain yogurt

2 tbsp freshly grated
Parmesan cheese

salt and pepper

TO GARNISH

shredded fresh basil leaves

fresh Parmesan cheese shavings

1 Put the mushrooms into a pan
with the bouillon. Bring to a boil
over a medium heat. Cover and cook
for 3–4 minutes, or until tender. Drain
and set aside. Set aside the cooking
liquid to use in soups if you wish.

2 Bring a small pan of water to a
boil over a medium heat. Add the
asparagus and cook for 3–4 minutes,
or until just tender. Drain and set aside
until required.

3 Bring a large pan of lightly salted
water to a boil over a medium
heat. Add the pasta and cook for about
8–10 minutes, or until done. Drain the
pasta thoroughly, return to the pan,
and keep warm.

4 Meanwhile, make the pesto. Put
all the ingredients into a blender
or food processor and process for a few
seconds until smooth. Alternatively,
finely chop the basil and mix all the
ingredients together in a small bowl.

5 Add the mushrooms, asparagus,
and artichoke hearts to the pasta
and cook, stirring for 2–3 minutes.

Remove from the heat and mix the
vegetables with the pesto.

6 Transfer to 4 large, warmed
bowls and garnish with fresh
basil and Parmesan cheese. Serve.

spaghetti & mushroom sauce

serves four

4 tbsp butter

1 tbsp olive oil

6 shallots, sliced

6 cups sliced white mushrooms

1 tsp all-purpose flour

⅝ cup heavy cream

2 tbsp port

½ cup sun-dried tomatoes, chopped

freshly grated nutmeg

1 lb/450 g dried spaghetti

1 tbsp chopped fresh parsley

salt and pepper

1 fresh parsley sprig, to garnish

6 triangles of fried white bread,
   to serve

1 Heat the butter and the oil in a pan over a medium heat. Add the shallots and cook for 3 minutes. Reduce the heat, add the mushrooms and cook for 2 minutes. Season and sprinkle over the flour. Cook, stirring, for 1 minute.

2 Gradually stir in the cream and port, then add the sun-dried tomatoes and a pinch of grated nutmeg, and cook over a low heat for 8 minutes.

3 Meanwhile, bring a large pan of lightly salted water to a boil over a medium heat. Add the pasta and cook for 12–14 minutes, or until done.

VARIATION

Non-vegetarians could add 4 oz/115 g prosciutto, cut into thin strips and heated gently in 2 tbsp butter, to the pasta with the mushroom sauce.

4 Drain the pasta and return to the pan. Pour over the mushroom sauce and cook for 3 minutes. Transfer the pasta to a large serving plate, sprinkle over the chopped parsley. Garnish with a parsley sprig and serve with crispy triangles of fried bread.

paglia e fieno

4 tbsp butter

1 lb/450 g fresh peas, shelled

⅞ cup heavy cream

1 lb/450 g mixed fresh green and
white spaghetti or tagliatelle

⅔ cup freshly grated
Parmesan cheese

pinch of freshly grated nutmeg

salt and pepper

fresh Parmesan cheese shavings,
to serve

VARIATION

Cook 2 cups sliced white or
exotic mushrooms in 4 tbsp of
butter over a low heat for
4–5 minutes. Stir into the peas
and cream sauce just before
adding to the pasta in step 4.

---

1 Melt the butter in a large pan over a low heat. Add the peas and cook for 2–3 minutes.

2 Using a measuring cup, pour ⅝ cup of the cream into the pan. Bring to a boil over a low heat and simmer for 1–1½ minutes, or until slightly thickened. Remove the pan from the heat.

3 Meanwhile, bring a large pan of lightly salted water to a boil over a medium heat. Add the pasta and cook for 2–3 minutes, or until done. Remove the pan from the heat and drain the pasta thoroughly, then return to the pan.

4 Add the peas and cream sauce to the pasta. Return the pan to the heat, then add the remaining cream and the Parmesan cheese and season to taste with salt, pepper, and freshly grated nutmeg.

5 Using 2 forks, gently toss the pasta to coat with the peas and cream sauce, while heating through.

6 Transfer the pasta to 4 warmed serving dish and serve with shavings of Parmesan cheese.

pasta with green vegetables

serves four

2 cups dried gemelli or other
    pasta shapes

1 head broccoli, cut into flowerets

2 zucchini, sliced

8 oz/225 g asparagus spears

4 oz/115 g snow peas

¾ cup frozen peas

2 tbsp butter

3 tbsp vegetable bouillon

4 tbsp heavy cream

freshly grated nutmeg

2 tbsp chopped fresh parsley

2 tbsp freshly grated
    Parmesan cheese

salt and pepper

1 Bring a large pan of lightly salted water to a boil over a medium heat. Add the pasta and cook until done. Drain thoroughly and return to the pan, cover and keep warm.

2 Steam the broccoli, zucchini, asparagus spears, and snow peas over a pan of boiling water until just softened. Remove from the heat and refresh in cold water. Drain. Set aside.

3 Bring a small pan of lightly salted water to a boil over a low heat. Add the peas and cook for 3 minutes. Drain and refresh in cold water, then drain again. Set aside with the other vegetables.

4 Heat the butter and bouillon into a pan over a medium heat. Add all of the vegetables, and set aside a few of the asparagus spears. Toss the vegetables carefully with a wooden spoon, until heated through, taking care not to break them up.

5 Stir in the cream and heat through without bringing to a boil. Season to taste with salt, pepper, and nutmeg.

6 Transfer the pasta to a warmed serving dish and stir in the parsley. Spoon over the sauce and sprinkle over the Parmesan cheese. Arrange the reserved asparagus spears in a pattern on top and serve.

italian tomato sauce & pasta

serves two

1 tbsp olive oil

1 small onion, chopped finely

1–2 garlic cloves, minced

350 g/12 oz tomatoes, peeled and chopped

2 tsp tomato paste

2 tbsp water

2½–3 cups dried pasta shapes

¾ cup lean bacon, derinded and diced

½ cup mushrooms, sliced

1 tbsp chopped fresh parsley or 1 tsp chopped fresh cilantro

2 tbsp sour cream, optional

salt and pepper

3 Meanwhile, bring a large pan of lightly salted water to a boil over a medium heat. Add the pasta and cook for 8–10 minutes, or until done. Drain the pasta thoroughly and transfer to 2 warmed serving dishes.

4 Heat the bacon gently in a skillet until the fat runs, then add the mushrooms and continue cooking for 3–4 minutes. Drain off any excess oil.

5 Add the bacon and mushrooms to the tomato mixture, together with the parsley or cilantro and the sour cream (if using). Heat through and serve with the pasta.

COOK'S TIP

Sour cream contains 18–20% fat, so if you are following a low-fat diet you can leave it out of this recipe or substitute a low-fat alternative.

1 To make the tomato sauce, heat the oil in a pan over a low heat. Add the onion and garlic and cook until soft.

2 Add the tomatoes, tomato paste, water. Season to taste with salt and pepper and bring to a boil. Cover and simmer gently for 10 minutes.

pasta & bean casserole

serves four

1¼ cups dried navy beans, soaked
  overnight and drained

2 cups dried penne

5 tbsp olive oil

3½ cups vegetable bouillon

2 large onions, sliced

2 garlic cloves, chopped

2 bay leaves

1 tsp dried oregano

1 tsp dried thyme

5 tbsp red wine

2 tbsp tomato paste

2 celery stalks, sliced

1 fennel bulb, sliced

1⅝ cups sliced mushrooms

8 oz/225 g tomatoes, sliced

1 tsp brown sugar

4 tbsp dry white bread crumbs

salt and pepper

TO SERVE

salad greens

crusty bread

1 Put the navy beans into a large pan and add enough cold water to cover. Bring to a boil over a high heat and boil rapidly for 20 minutes. Drain, set aside, and keep warm.

2 Bring a large pan of lightly salted water to a boil over a medium heat. Add the pasta and cook for about 3 minutes, or until done. Drain thoroughly. Set aside and keep warm.

3 Put the beans into a large, flameproof casserole dish. Add the vegetable bouillon and stir in the oil, the onions, garlic, bay leaves, oregano, thyme, wine, and tomato paste. Bring to a boil over a medium heat. Cover and cook in a preheated oven at 350°F/180°C, for 2 hours.

4 Add the pasta, celery, fennel, mushrooms, and tomatoes to the casserole and season to taste with salt and pepper. Stir in the brown sugar and sprinkle over the bread crumbs. Cover the casserole and cook in the oven for 1 hour.

5 Transfer to 4 large serving bowls and serve immediately with salad greens and crusty bread.

spinach & exotic mushroom lasagna

serves four

8 tbsp butter, plus extra for greasing

2 garlic cloves, chopped finely

4 oz/115 g shallots

8 oz/225 g exotic mushrooms, such
   as chanterelles

1 cup spinach, cooked, drained, and
   chopped finely

2 cups freshly grated cheddar cheese

¼ tsp freshly grated nutmeg

1 tsp chopped fresh basil

4 tbsp all-purpose flour

2½ cups hot milk

⅔ cup freshly grated
   Cheshire cheese

salt and pepper

8 sheets precooked lasagna

1 Lightly grease an ovenproof dish
with a little butter.

2 Melt 4 tablespoons of the butter
in a pan over a low heat. Add the
garlic, shallots, and exotic mushrooms
and cook for 3 minutes. Stir in the
spinach, hard cheese, nutmeg, and
basil. Season to taste with salt and
pepper, then set aside.

3 Melt the remaining butter in
another pan over a low heat. Add
the flour and cook, stirring constantly,
for 1 minute. Gradually stir in the hot
milk, whisking constantly, until smooth.
Stir in ¼ cup of the Cheshire cheese
and season to taste.

4 Spread half the mushroom
mixture over the bottom of
the prepared dish. Cover with a layer
of lasagna, then with half the cheese
sauce. Repeat the process and sprinkle
over the remaining cheese. Cook in a
preheated oven at 400°F/200°C, for
30 minutes, or until golden brown.
Transfer to 4 serving plates and serve.

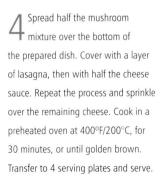

penne & vegetables

serves four

2 cups dried penne

2 tbsp olive oil

2 tbsp butter

2 garlic cloves, minced

1 green bell pepper, seeded and
   sliced thinly

1 yellow bell pepper, seeded and
   sliced thinly

16 cherry tomatoes, halved

1 tbsp chopped oregano

½ cup dry white wine

2 tbsp pitted ripe black olives, cut
   into fourths

2¾ oz/75 g arugula

salt and pepper

fresh oregano sprigs, to garnish

VARIATION

If arugula is unavailable, spinach
makes a good substitute. Follow
the same cooking instructions
as for arugula.

1 Bring a pan of lightly salted water
to a boil over a medium heat.
Add the pasta and cook for about
8–10 minutes, or until done. Drain the
pasta thoroughly.

2 Heat the oil and butter in a pan
over a low heat. Add the garlic
and cook for 30 seconds. Add the bell
peppers and cook, stirring occasionally,
for 3–4 minutes.

3 Stir in the tomatoes, oregano,
wine, and olives and cook for
3–4 minutes. Season and stir in the
arugula until just wilted.

4 Transfer to a serving dish, spoon
over the sauce and garnish with
an oregano sprig. Serve.

vegetables & beancurd

serves four

8 oz/225 g asparagus spears

4 oz/115 g snow peas

8 oz/225 g green beans

1 leek

8 oz/225 g shelled small fava beans

2¾ cups dried fusilli

2 tbsp olive oil

2 tbsp butter

1 garlic clove, minced

8 oz/225 g beancurd, cut into
  1-inch/2.5-cm cubes
  (drained weight)

½ cup pitted green olives in
  brine, drained

salt and pepper

freshly grated Parmesan cheese,
  to serve

1 Using a sharp knife, cut the asparagus into 2-inch/5-cm lengths. Thinly slice the snow peas diagonally and slice the green beans into 1-inch/2.5-cm pieces. Thinly slice the leek and set aside until required.

2 Bring a large pan of water to a boil over a medium heat. Add the asparagus, green beans, and fava beans and cook for 5 minutes. Drain thoroughly, rinse in cold water, and drain again. Set aside.

3 Bring a large pan of lightly salted water to a boil over a medium heat. Add the pasta and cook for about 8–10 minutes, or until done. Drain the pasta thoroughly. Toss in 1 tablespoon of the oil and season to taste with salt and pepper.

4 Meanwhile, heat a wok over a low heat. Add the remaining oil and the butter and when hot, add the leek, garlic, and beancurd and cook for 1–2 minutes, or until the vegetables have just softened.

5 Stir in the snow peas and cook for an additional minute.

6 Add the blanched vegetables and olives to the wok and heat through for 1 minute. Carefully stir in the pasta and adjust the seasoning, if necessary. Cook for 1 minute and pile into a warmed serving dish. Serve with Parmesan cheese.

vegetable cannelloni

serves four

1 eggplant

½ cup olive oil

1 cup fresh spinach

2 garlic cloves, minced

1 tsp ground cumin

1¼ cups chopped mushrooms

12 cannelloni tubes

salt and pepper

TOMATO SAUCE

1 tbsp olive oil

1 onion, chopped

2 garlic cloves, crushed

1 lb 12 oz/800 g canned

    chopped tomatoes

1 tsp superfine sugar

2 tbsp chopped fresh basil

2 oz/55 g sliced mozzarella cheese

1 Cut the eggplant into small dice. Heat the oil in a skillet over a medium heat. Add the eggplant and cook, stirring frequently, for about 2–3 minutes.

2 Add the spinach, garlic, cumin, and mushrooms and reduce the heat. Season to taste with salt and pepper and cook, stirring constantly, for 2–3 minutes. Spoon the mixture into the cannelloni tubes and arrange in a casserole in a single layer.

3 To make the sauce, heat the oil in a pan over a medium heat. Add the onion and garlic and cook for 1 minute. Add the tomatoes, sugar, and basil and bring to a boil. Reduce the heat and simmer gently for about 5 minutes. Spoon the sauce over the cannelloni tubes.

4 Arrange the sliced mozzarella cheese on top of the sauce and cook in a preheated oven at 375°F/ 190°C, for about 30 minutes, or until the cheese is golden brown and bubbling. Serve immediately.

macaroni cheese & tomato

serves four

2 cups dried elbow-macaroni

1½ cups freshly grated
   cheddar cheese

generous 1 cup freshly grated
   Parmesan cheese

1 tbsp butter, plus extra for greasing

4 tbsp fresh white bread crumbs

1 tbsp chopped fresh basil

salt and pepper

TOMATO SAUCE

1 tbsp olive oil

1 shallot, chopped finely

2 garlic cloves, minced

1 lb 2 oz/500 g canned
   chopped tomatoes

1 tbsp chopped fresh basil

1 To make the tomato sauce, heat the oil in a pan over a medium heat. Add the shallots and garlic and cook, stirring constantly, for 1 minute. Add the tomatoes and basil, and season to taste with salt and pepper. Cook, stirring, for 10 minutes.

2 Meanwhile, bring a large pan of lightly salted water to a boil over a medium heat. Add the macaroni and cook for 8 minutes, or until done. Drain the macaroni thoroughly.

3 Mix the grated cheddar and Parmesan cheeses together in a bowl. Grease a deep casserole dish. Spoon one-third of the tomato sauce into the bottom of the dish, cover with one-third of the macaroni, then top with one-third of the mixed cheeses. Season to taste with salt and pepper. Repeat these layers twice, ending with a layer of grated cheeses.

4 Mix the bread crumbs and basil together and sprinkle evenly over the top. Dot the topping with the butter and cook in a preheated oven at 375°F/190°C, for 25 minutes, or until the topping is golden brown and bubbling. Serve immediately.

217

zucchini & eggplant lasagna

serves four

2 lb 4 oz/1 kg eggplant

8 tbsp olive oil

2 tbsp garlic and herb butter

1 lb/450 g zucchini, sliced

2 cups freshly grated
   mozzarella cheese

2½ cups strained tomatoes

6 sheets precooked green lasagna

2½ cups Bechamel Sauce
   (see page 98)

⅔ cup freshly grated
   Parmesan cheese

1 tsp dried oregano

salt and pepper

1 Thinly slice the eggplant and put in a strainer. Sprinkle with salt and set aside for 20 minutes. Rinse and pat dry on paper towels.

2 Heat 4 tablespoons of the oil in a large skillet over a low heat. Add half the eggplant slices and cook for 6–7 minutes, or until golden. Drain well on paper towels. Repeat with the remaining oil and eggplant. Set aside.

3 Melt the garlic and herb butter in the skillet. Add the zucchini and cook for 5–6 minutes, or until golden brown. Drain on paper towels.

4 Put half the cooked eggplant and zucchini slices into a large ovenproof dish. Season with pepper and sprinkle over half the mozzarella cheese. Spoon over half the strained tomatoes and top with 3 sheets of lasagna. Repeat the process, ending with a layer of lasagna.

5 Spoon over the Bechamel Sauce (see page 98) and sprinkle over the Parmesan cheese and oregano. Put the dish on a cookie sheet and cook in a preheated oven at 425°F/220°C, for 30–35 minutes, or until golden brown. Serve immediately.

pasta with garlic & broccoli

serves four

1 lb 2 oz/500 g broccoli

1⅓ cups garlic and herb
    cream cheese

4 tbsp milk

12 oz/350 g fresh herb tagliatelle

⅓ cup freshly grated
    Parmesan cheese

salt

snipped fresh chives, to garnish

1 Cut the broccoli into even-size flowerets. Bring a pan of lightly salted water to a boil over a medium heat. Add the broccoli and cook for 3 minutes, then drain thoroughly.

2 Put the soft cheese into a pan and warm over a low heat, stirring constantly, until melted. Add the milk and stir until well blended.

3 Add the cooked broccoli to the cheese mixture and, using a wooden spoon, stir to coat.

4 Meanwhile, bring a large pan of lightly salted water to a boil over a medium heat. Add the pasta and cook for 3–4 minutes, or until done.

5 Drain the pasta thoroughly and transfer to 4 warmed serving plates. Spoon the broccoli and cheese sauce on top. Sprinkle with grated Parmesan cheese, garnish with snipped chives, and serve immediately.

creamy pasta & broccoli

serves four

4 tbsp butter

1 large onion, chopped finely

1 lb/450 g dried ribbon pasta

1 lb/450 g broccoli, broken
　　into flowerets

⅝ cup boiling vegetable bouillon

1 tbsp all-purpose flour

⅝ cup light cream

½ cup freshly grated
　　mozzarella cheese

freshly grated nutmeg

salt and white pepper

fresh apple slices, to garnish

1 Melt half of the butter in a large pan over a medium heat. Add the onion and cook for 4 minutes.

2 Add the broccoli and pasta to the pan and cook, stirring constantly, for 2 minutes. Add the bouillon, bring back to a boil and simmer for an additional 12 minutes. Season well with salt and white pepper.

3 Meanwhile, melt the remaining butter in a pan over a medium eat. Sprinkle over the flour and cook,

stirring constantly, for 2 minutes. Gradually stir in the cream and bring to simmering point, but do not boil. Add the grated cheese and season with salt and a little freshly grated nutmeg.

4 Drain the pasta and broccoli mixture and return to the pan. Pour over the cheese sauce and cook, stirring occasionally, for about 2 minutes. Transfer the pasta and broccoli mixture to a large, warmed serving dish and garnish with a few slices of apple. Serve.

mediterranean spaghetti

serves four

1 tbsp olive oil

1 large, red onion, chopped

2 garlic cloves, minced

1 tbsp lemon juice

4 baby eggplant, cut into fourths

2½ cups strained tomatoes

2 tsp superfine sugar

2 tbsp tomato paste

14 oz/400 g canned artichoke
    hearts, drained and halved

1 cup pitted ripe black olives

12 oz/350 g dried spaghetti

2 tbsp butter

salt and pepper

fresh basil sprigs, to garnish

olive bread, to serve

1 Heat 1 tablespoon of the oil into a large skillet over a low heat. Add the onion, garlic, lemon juice, and eggplant and cook for 4–5 minutes, or until the onion and eggplant are lightly golden brown.

2 Pour in the strained tomatoes, season to taste with salt and pepper and stir in the superfine sugar, and tomato paste. Bring to a boil, then reduce the heat and simmer, stirring occasionally, for 20 minutes.

3 Gently stir in the artichoke hearts and olives, then cook for an additional 5 minutes.

4 Meanwhile, bring a large pan of lightly salted water to a boil over a medium heat. Add the pasta and cook for 7–8 minutes, or until done.

5 Drain the pasta thoroughly and toss with the butter. Transfer the pasta to a large, warmed serving dish.

6 Pour the vegetable sauce over the pasta. Transfer to 4 warmed serving plates and garnish with the basil sprigs. Serve with olive bread.

green tagliatelle with garlic

serves four

2 tbsp walnut oil

1 bunch scallions, sliced

2 garlic cloves, sliced thinly

3¼ cups sliced mushrooms

1 lb/450 g fresh green and
   white tagliatelle

1¼ cups frozen spinach, thawed,
   and drained

½ cup full-fat soft cheese flavored
   with garlic and herbs

4 tbsp light cream

½ cup chopped, unsalted
   pistachio nuts

2 tbsp shredded fresh basil

salt and pepper

fresh basil sprigs, to garnish

1 Heat the walnut oil in a large skillet over a low heat. Add the scallions and garlic and cook for 1 minute, or until just softened.

2 Add the mushrooms to the skillet and stir well. Cover and cook for about 5 minutes, or until softened.

3 Meanwhile, bring a large pan of lightly salted water to a boil over a medium heat. Add the pasta and cook for 3–5 minutes, or until done. Drain the pasta thoroughly and return to the pan.

4 Add the spinach to the skillet with the mushrooms and heat through for 1–2 minutes. Add the cheese to the skillet and let melt slightly. Stir in the cream and continue to cook, without letting the mixture come to a boil, until the mixture is warmed through.

5 Pour the sauce over the pasta, then season to taste with salt and pepper and mix well. Heat throug gently, stirring constantly, for about 2–3 minutes.

6 Transfer the pasta to a large serving dish and sprinkle with th pistachio nuts and shredded basil. Garnish with basil sprigs and serve.

pasta & vegetable sauce

serves four

3 tbsp olive oil

1 onion, sliced

2 garlic cloves, chopped

3 red bell peppers, seeded and cut
  into strips

3 zucchini, sliced

14 oz/400 g canned
  chopped tomatoes

3 tbsp sun-dried tomato paste

2 tbsp chopped fresh basil

2 cups fresh fusilli

1 cup freshly grated Swiss cheese

salt and pepper

fresh basil sprigs, to garnish

3 Meanwhile, bring a large pan of lightly salted water to a boil over a medium heat. Add the pasta and cook for 3 minutes, or until done. Drain the pasta thoroughly and add to the vegetable mixture. Toss gently to mix well.

4 Transfer to a shallow flameproof dish and sprinkle with the cheese.

5 Cook under a preheated hot broiler for 5 minutes, until the cheese is golden brown and bubbling. Transfer to 4 large, warmed serving plates, garnish with basil sprigs and serve immediately.

1 Heat the oil in a heavy-bottomed pan or flameproof casserole dish ver a medium heat. Add the onion d garlic and cook until softened. Add e bell peppers and zucchini, then ok for 5 minutes.

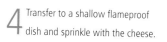

2 Add the tomatoes, sun-dried tomato paste, and basil, and ason to taste with salt and pepper. ver and cook for 5 minutes.

homemade noodles

serves two-four

NOODLES

¾ cup all-purpose flour

2 tbsp cornstarch

½ tsp salt

½ cup boiling water

5 tbsp vegetable oil

STIR-FRY

1 zucchini, cut into thin sticks

1 celery stick, cut into thin sticks

1 carrot, cut into thin sticks

1 cup open-cup mushrooms, sliced

4½ oz/125 g broccoli flowerets and
    stalks, peeled, and sliced thinly

1 leek, sliced

4½ oz/125 g bean sprouts

1 tbsp soy sauce

2 tsp rice wine vinegar

½ tsp sugar

1 To prepare the noodles, sift the flour, cornstarch, and salt into a bowl. Make a well in the center and pour in the boiling water and 1 teaspoon of oil. Mix quickly to make a soft dough. Cover and let stand for 5–6 minutes.

2 Make the noodles by breaking off small pieces of dough and rolling into balls. Roll each ball across a very lightly oiled counter with the palm of your hand to form thin noodles. Do not worry if some of the noodles break into shorter lengths. Set the noodles aside until required.

3 Heat a large wok over a high heat. Add 3 tablespoons of the vegetable oil and when hot, add the noodles, in batches, and cook for 1 minute. Reduce the heat and cook for an additional 2 minutes. Remove and drain on paper towels. Set aside.

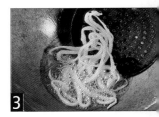

4 Heat the remaining oil in the wok. Add the zucchini, celery, and carrot, and cook, stirring, for 1 minute. Add the mushrooms, broccoli, and leek, and cook, stirring, for 1 minute.

5 Add the bean sprouts, soy sauce, rice wine vinegar, and sugar to the wok and mix until heated through.

6 Add the noodles and cook until heated through, tossing with 2 forks to mix the ingredients. Serve.

pear & walnut pasta

serves four

8 oz/225 g dried spaghetti

2 small ripe pears, peeled and sliced

⅔ cup vegetable bouillon

6 tbsp dry white wine

2 tbsp butter

1 tbsp olive oil

1 red onion, sliced

1 garlic clove, minced

½ cup walnut halves

2 tbsp chopped fresh oregano

1 tbsp lemon juice

3 oz/85 g dolcelatte cheese

salt and pepper

fresh oregano sprigs, to garnish

1 Bring a large pan of lightly salted water to a boil over a medium heat. Add the pasta and cook for 8–10 minutes, or until done. Drain the pasta thoroughly, set aside, and keep warm until required.

2 Meanwhile, put the pears into a pan and pour in the bouillon and wine. Poach the pears over a low heat for about 10 minutes, or until tender. Remove the pears with a slotted spoon and set aside the cooking liquid. Set the pears aside.

3 Heat the butter and oil in a pan over a low heat. Add the onion and garlic, then cook, stirring frequently, for 2–3 minutes.

4 Stir in the walnut halves, chopped oregano, and lemon juice. Stir in the reserved pears with 4 tablespoons of the poaching liquid.

5 Crumble the dolcelatte cheese into the pan and cook over a low heat, stirring occasionally, for about 1–2 minutes, or until the cheese is just starting to melt. Season to taste with salt and pepper.

6 Add the pasta and, using 2 forks toss in the sauce. Transfer to a large serving dish, garnish with oregano sprigs, and serve.

traditional cannelloni

serves four

20 tubes dried cannelloni (about
    7 oz/200 g) or 20 square sheets
    of fresh pasta (12 oz/350 g)
generous 1 cup ricotta cheese
1 cup frozen spinach, thawed
½ small red bell pepper, seeded
    and diced
2 scallions, chopped
1 tbsp butter for greasing
⅔ cup hot vegetable bouillon
1 quantity Tomato Sauce
    (see page 216),
⅓ cup freshly grated Parmesan or
    romano cheese
salt and pepper

1 If necessary, precook the dried
    cannelloni. Bring a large pan of
water to a boil over a medium heat.
Add the pasta and cook for about
3–4 minutes. It may be easier to cook
the cannelloni in batches.

2 Mix the ricotta, spinach, bell
    pepper, and scallions together in
a bowl and season to taste with salt
and pepper.

3 Lightly grease a large casserole,
    with a little butter. Spoon the
ricotta mixture into the pasta tubes and
put them into the prepared dish in a
single layer. If using fresh sheets of
pasta, spread the ricotta mixture along
one side of each fresh pasta square
and roll up to form a tube.

4 Mix the stock and tomato sauce
    together and pour it over the
cannelloni tubes.

5 Sprinkle the grated Parmesan or
    romano cheese evenly over the
cannelloni and cook in a preheated
oven at 375°F/190°C, for about
20–25 minutes, or until the cannelloni
is cooked through and the topping
is golden brown and bubbling.
Serve immediately.

tortelloni

10½ oz/300 g thin sheets of
    fresh pasta

5 tbsp butter

1¾ oz/50 g shallots, chopped finely

3 garlic cloves, minced

½ cup mushrooms, chopped finely

½ celery stalk, chopped finely

¼ cup finely grated romano cheese,
    plus extra to garnish

salt and pepper

1 Using a serrated pasta cutter, cut 2-inch/5-cm squares from the sheets of fresh pasta. To make 36 tortelloni, you will need 72 squares. Once the pasta is cut, cover with plastic wrap to stop them drying out.

2 Heat 3 tablespoons of the butter in a large skillet over a low heat. Add the shallots, 1 garlic clove, mushrooms, and celery, and cook for 4–5 minutes.

3 Remove the skillet from the heat, then stir in the cheese and season to taste with salt and pepper.

4 Spoon ½ teaspoon of the mixture onto the center of 36 pasta squares. Brush the edges of the squares with water and top with the remaining 36 squares. Press the edges together to seal. Let rest for 5 minutes.

5 Bring a large pan of lightly salted water to a boil over a medium heat. Add the tortelloni, in batches, and cook for 2–3 minutes. The tortelloni will rise to the surface when cooked and the pasta should be tender. Remove from the pan with a slotted spoon and drain thoroughly.

6 Meanwhile, melt the remaining butter in a pan. Add the remaining garlic and plenty of pepper and cook for 1–2 minutes.

7 Transfer the tortelloni to 4 servin plates and pour over the garlic butter. Garnish with grated romano cheese and serve immediately.

spinach & nut pasta

serves four

2 cups dried pasta shapes

½ cup olive oil

2 garlic cloves, minced

1 onion, sliced

3 large flat mushrooms, sliced

1 cup frozen spinach

2 tbsp pine nuts

5 tbsp dry white wine

salt and pepper

fresh Parmesan cheese shavings,
    to garnish

COOK'S TIP

Grate a little nutmeg over
the dish for extra flavor, because
this spice has a particular
affinity with spinach.

1   Bring a large pan of lightly salted
    water to a boil over a medium
heat. Add the pasta and cook for about
8–10 minutes, or until done. Drain the
pasta thoroughly.

2   Meanwhile, heat the oil in a large
    pan over a low heat. Add the
garlic and onion and cook, stirring
occasionally, for 1 minute.

3   Add the mushrooms to the pan
    and cook over a medium heat,
stirring occasionally, for 2 minutes.

4   Reduce the heat, add the spinach,
    and cook, stirring occasionally, for
about 4–5 minutes, or until the
spinach has just wilted.

5   Stir in the pine nuts and wine,
    season to taste with salt and
pepper, and cook for 1 minute.

6   Transfer the pasta to a warmed
    serving bowl and toss the sauce
into it, mixing well. Garnish with
shavings of Parmesan cheese and
serve immediately.

eggplant & penne bake

serves four

2 cups dried penne or other short
    pasta shapes

3 tbsp olive oil, plus extra
    for brushing

2 eggplant

1 large onion, chopped

2 garlic cloves, minced

14 oz/400 g canned
    chopped tomatoes

2 tsp dried oregano

2 oz/55 g mozzarella cheese,
    sliced thinly

⅓ cup freshly grated
    Parmesan cheese

2 tbsp dry bread crumbs

salt and pepper

salad greens, to serve

1 Bring a pan of lightly salted water to a boil over a medium heat. Add the pasta and cook until done. Drain the pasta thoroughly and return to the pan, cover and keep warm.

2 Cut the eggplant in half lengthwise and score around the inside with a sharp knife, being careful not to pierce the shells. Scoop out the flesh with a spoon. Brush the insides of the shells generously with oil. Chop the flesh and set aside.

3 Heat the remaining oil in a skillet over a low heat. Add the onion and cook until translucent. Add the garlic and cook for 1 minute. Add the chopped eggplant and cook, stirring frequently, for 5 minutes. Add the tomatoes and oregano, and season to taste with salt and pepper. Bring to a boil and simmer for 10 minutes, or until thickened. Remove from the heat and stir in the pasta.

4 Brush a cookie sheet with oil and arrange the eggplant shells in a single layer. Divide half the tomato and pasta mixture between them. Sprinkle over the mozzarella cheese, then pile the remaining tomato and pasta mixture on top. Mix the Parmesan cheese and bread crumbs together and sprinkle over the top.

5 Cook in a preheated oven at 400°F/200°C, for 25 minutes, or until the topping is golden brown. Serve with salad greens.

fried vegetable noodles

serves four

12 oz/350 g dried egg noodles

2 tbsp groundnut oil

2 garlic cloves, minced

½ tsp ground star anise

1 carrot, cut into very thin sticks

1 green bell pepper, cut into very
thin sticks

1 onion, sliced

4½ oz/125 g broccoli flowerets

2¾ oz/75 g canned bamboo shoots

1 celery stalk, sliced

1 tbsp light soy sauce

⅔ cup vegetable bouillon

1¼ cups oil for deep-frying

1 tsp cornstarch

2 tsp water

1 Bring a large pan of water to a boil over a medium heat. Add the noodles and cook for 1–2 minutes. Drain thoroughly and rinse under cold running water. Let the noodles drain thoroughly in a strainer until required.

2 Heat a wok over a high heat. Add the oil and when smoking, reduce the heat, add the garlic and ground star anise, and cook for 30 seconds. Add the remaining vegetables and cook for 1–2 minutes.

3 Add the soy sauce and vegetable bouillon to the wok and cook over a low heat for 5 minutes.

4 Heat another wok over a high heat. Add the oil for deep-frying and heat to 350°F/180°C, or until a cube of bread browns in 30 seconds.

5 Using a fork, twist the drained noodles and form them into rounds. Deep-fry them, in batches, until crisp, turning once. Let drain on paper towels.

6 Blend the cornstarch with the water to form a paste and stir into the vegetables. Bring to a boil over a medium heat, stirring constantly, until the sauce is thickened.

7 Arrange the noodles onto 4 large serving plates, spoon the vegetables on top, and serve.

macaroni & corn crêpes

serves four

2 corn cobs

4 tbsp butter

4 oz/115 g red bell peppers, seeded
and diced finely

2½ cups dried short-cut macaroni

⅝ cup heavy cream

¼ cup all-purpose flour

4 egg yolks

4 tbsp olive oil

salt and pepper

TO SERVE

exotic mushrooms

cooked leeks

1 Bring a pan of water to a boil over a medium heat. Add the corn and cook for about 8 minutes. Drain thoroughly and refresh under cold running water for 3 minutes. Carefully cut away the kernels onto paper towels and set aside to dry.

2 Melt 2 tablespoons of the butter in a skillet over a low heat. Add the peppers and cook for 4 minutes. Drain and pat dry on paper towels.

3 Bring a large pan of lightly salted water to a boil over a medium heat. Add the macaroni and cook for 12 minutes, or until done. Drain the macaroni thoroughly and let cool in cold water until required.

4 Beat the cream, flour, a pinch of salt, and the egg yolks together in a bowl until smooth. Add the corn and bell peppers to the cream and egg mixture. Drain the macaroni, then toss into the corn and cream mixture. Season well with pepper.

5 Heat the remaining butter with the oil in a large skillet over a medium heat. Drop spoonfuls of the mixture into the skillet and press down until the mixture forms a flat crêpe. Cook until golden on both sides, and until all the mixture is used. Serve immediately with exotic mushrooms and cooked leeks.

macaroni bake

1 Bring a large pan of lightly salted water to a boil over a medium heat. Add the macaroni and cook for about 12 minutes, or until done. Drain the macaroni thoroughly and set aside.

2 Melt the butter in a large flameproof casserole dish over a medium heat, then remove the dish from the heat.

3 Make alternate layers of potatoes, onions, macaroni, and grated cheese in the dish, seasoning well with salt and pepper between each layer and finishing with a layer of cheese on top. Finally, pour over the cream.

4 Cook in a preheated oven at 400°F/200°C, for 25 minutes. Remove the dish from the oven and put under a preheated medium-hot broiler to brown the top of the bake.

5 Serve the bake straight from the dish with crusty brown bread and butter as a main course. Alternatively, serve as a vegetable accompaniment with your favorite main course.

vegetable pasta stir-fry

serves four

3½ cups dried whole-wheat pasta
shells or other short pasta shapes

2 carrots, sliced thinly

4 oz/115 g baby corn cobs

3 tbsp corn oil

1-inch/2.5-cm piece fresh
gingerroot, sliced thinly

1 large onion, sliced thinly

1 garlic clove, sliced thinly

3 celery stalks, sliced thinly

1 small red bell pepper, seeded
and cut into short, thin sticks

1 small green bell pepper, seeded
and cut into short, thin sticks

1 tsp cornstarch

2 tbsp water

3 tbsp soy sauce

3 tbsp dry sherry

1 tsp honey

dash of hot pepper sauce, optional

salt

1 Bring a large pan of lightly salted water to a boil over a medium heat. Add the pasta and cook for about 8–10 minutes, or until done. Drain, then return to the pan and keep warm.

2 Bring a pan of lightly salted water to a boil over a medium heat. Add the carrots and corn and cook for 2 minutes. Drain, then refresh in cold water and drain again.

3 Heat a large wok over a medium heat. Add the corn oil and when hot, add the ginger and cook, stirring, for about 1 minute to flavor the oil. Remove the ginger with a slotted spoon and discard.

4 Add the onion, garlic, celery, and bell peppers to the wok and cook for 2 minutes. Add the carrots and baby corn and cook for 2 minutes. Stir in the strained pasta.

5 Mix the cornstarch and water together to make a smooth paste. Stir in the soy sauce, sherry, and honey. Pour the cornstarch mixture into the pasta and cook, stirring occasionally, for 2 minutes. Stir in a dash of pepper sauce (if using). Transfer to a serving dish and serve immediately.

three-cheese macaroni

serves four

2½ cups béchamel sauce
   (see page 98)

2 cups dried macaroni

1 tbsp oil, for oiling

1 egg, beaten

1 cup freshly grated cheddar cheese

1 tbsp whole-grain mustard

2 tbsp snipped fresh chives

4 tomatoes, sliced

1 cup freshly grated brick cheese

½ cup freshly grated blue cheese

2 tbsp sunflower seeds

salt and pepper

snipped fresh chives, to garnish

1 Make the béchamel sauce (see page 98), transfer it into a bowl, and cover with plastic wrap to prevent a skin forming on the surface of the sauce. Set aside.

2 Bring a large pan of salted water to a boil over a medium heat. Add the macaroni and cook until just done. Drain thoroughly and put into a lightly oiled ovenproof dish.

3 Stir the beaten egg, cheddar cheese, mustard, and chives into the Béchamel Sauce and season to taste with salt and pepper.

4 Spoon the sauce over the macaroni, making sure it is well covered. Arrange the sliced tomatoes in a layer over the top.

5 Sprinkle the brick and blue cheeses, and the sunflower seeds evenly over the pasta bake. Put the dish onto a cookie sheet and cook in a preheated oven at 375°F/190°C, for 25–30 minutes, or until the topping is golden and bubbling.

6 Garnish the bake with snipped chives and serve immediately.

pasta mayo salad

serves four

1 large lettuces
2¼ cups dried penne
8 red eating apples
juice of 4 lemons
1 head celery, sliced
¾ cup shelled, halved walnuts
1⅛ cups fresh mayonnaise
salt

COOK'S TIP

Sprinkling the apples with lemon juice will prevent them from turning brown.

1 Wash, drain, and pat dry the lettuce leaves on paper towels. Transfer them to the refrigerator for hour, until crisp.

2 Meanwhile, bring a large pan of lightly salted water to a boil over medium heat. Add the pasta and ook until just done. Drain the pasta oroughly and refresh in cold water. rain again and set aside.

3 Core and dice the apples, then put them into a small bowl and sprinkle with the lemon juice. Mix the pasta, celery, apples, and walnuts together and toss the mixture in the mayonnaise. Add more mayonnaise, if you wish.

4 Line a large salad bowl with the lettuce leaves and spoon the pasta salad into the lined bowl. Serve when required.

vermicelli flan

serves four

225 g/8 oz dried vermicelli
    or spaghetti
2 tbsp butter, plus extra for greasing
salt and pepper
tomato and basil salad, to serve
SAUCE
½ stick butter
1 onion, chopped
5½ oz/150 g white
    mushrooms, trimmed
1 green bell pepper, seeded and
    sliced into thin rings
⅔ cup milk
3 eggs, beaten lightly
2 tbsp heavy cream
1 tsp dried oregano
pinch of finely grated nutmeg
1 tbsp freshly grated
    Parmesan cheese

1 Bring a large pan of lightly salted water to a boil over a medium heat. Add the pasta and cook for 8–10 minutes, or until done. Drain the pasta thoroughly, return to the pan, add the butter and shake the pan well.

2 Grease a 8-inch/20-cm loose-bottomed flan pan. Press the pasta onto the bottom and around the sides to form a case.

3 Heat the butter in a skillet over a medium heat. Add the onion and cook until it is translucent. Remove with a slotted spoon and spread in the flan case.

4 Add the mushrooms and bell pepper rings to the pan and turn them in the fat until glazed. Cook for 2 minutes on each side, then arrange in the flan case.

5 Beat the milk, eggs and cream together. Stir in the oregano, and season with nutmeg and pepper. Pour the mixture carefully over the vegetables and sprinkle with cheese.

6 Cook the flan in a preheated oven at 350°F/180°C, for about 40–45 minutes, or until the filling is set. Slide onto a serving plate and serve with a tomato and basil salad.

noodles with mushrooms

serves four

8 oz/225 g rice stick noodles

2 tbsp groundnut oil

1 garlic clove, chopped finely

¾-inch/2-cm piece fresh gingerroot, chopped finely

4 shallots, sliced thinly

1 cup sliced shiitake mushrooms

3½ oz/100 g firm beancurd, cut into ⅝-inch/1.5-cm dice (drained weight)

2 tbsp light soy sauce

1 tbsp rice wine

1 tbsp Thai fish sauce

1 tbsp smooth peanut butter

1 tsp chili sauce

2 tbsp toasted peanuts, chopped

shredded fresh basil leaves, to serve

COOK'S TIP

For an easy pantry dish, replace the shiitake mushrooms with a can of Chinese straw mushrooms. Alternatively, use dried shiitake mushrooms, soaked and drained before use.

1 Soak the rice stick noodles in hot water for 15 minutes, or according to the package instructions. Drain the noodles thoroughly.

2 Heat the oil in a skillet over a medium heat. Add the garlic, ginger, and shallots and cook for about 1–2 minutes, or until softened and lightly browned.

3 Add the mushrooms and cook for an additional 2–3 minutes. Stir in the beancurd and toss to brown lightly.

4 Mix the soy sauce, rice wine, fish sauce, peanut butter, and chili sauce together, then stir into the skillet.

5 Stir in the rice noodles and toss to coat evenly in the sauce. Transfer to a large serving dish and sprinkle with the peanuts and basil. Serve.

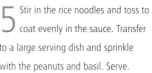

hot & sour noodles

serves four

9 oz/250 g dried medium
   egg noodles

1 tbsp sesame oil

1 tbsp chili oil

1 garlic clove, minced

2 scallions, chopped finely

scant 1 cup sliced white mushrooms

1½ oz/40 g dried Chinese black
   mushrooms, soaked, drained,
   and sliced

2 tbsp lime juice

3 tbsp light soy sauce

1 tsp sugar

shredded Napa cabbage, to serve

TO GARNISH

2 tbsp chopped fresh cilantro

2 tbsp toasted peanuts, chopped

COOK'S TIP

Thai chili oil is very hot, so if
you want a milder flavor, use
vegetable oil for the initial
cooking instead, then add
a final drizzle of chili oil just
for seasoning.

1 Bring a large pan of water to a
boil over a medium heat. Add the
noodles and cook for 3–4 minutes, or
according to the package instructions.
Drain thoroughly, return to the pan,
toss with the sesame oil, and set aside.

2 Heat the chili oil in a large skillet
over a medium heat. Add the
garlic, onions, and white mushrooms
and quickly cook for 2 minutes, or until
just softened.

3 Add the black mushrooms, lime
juice, soy sauce, and sugar and
continue cooking until boiling. Add the
noodles and toss to mix.

4 Make a bed of shredded Napa
cabbage on a large serving plate
and spoon the noodle mixture on top.
Garnish with the the cilantro and
peanuts and serve immediately.

Desserts

If when you think about cooking with pasta,
desserts do not usually spring to the forefront
of your mind, you will be amazed by the
wonderfully self-indulgent sweet pasta treats in this chapter.

The Italians love their desserts, but when there is a special gathering or

celebration, then a special effort is made and the delicacies appear. The

Sicilians are said to have the sweetest tooth of all, and many of the greatest

and most delicious Italian desserts are thought to have originated there.

honey & nut nests

serves four

8 oz/225 g dried angel hair pasta

½ cup butter

1½ cups chopped pistachio nuts

½ cup sugar

⅓ cup honey

⅔ cup water

2 tsp lemon juice

salt

strained plain yogurt, to serve

COOK'S TIP

Angel hair pasta is also known as capelli d'angelo. Long and very fine, it is usually sold in small bunches that already resemble nests.

1 Bring a large pan of lightly salted water to a boil over a medium heat. Add the pasta and cook for about 8–10 minutes, or until done. Drain the pasta thoroughly and return to the pan. Add the butter and toss to coat the pasta thoroughly. Let cool.

2 Arrange 4 small tart or poaching rings on a cookie sheet. Divide the angel hair pasta into 8 equal quantities and spoon 4 of them into the rings. Press down lightly with a spoon. Top the pasta with half the nuts, then add the remaining pasta.

3 Cook in a preheated oven at 350°F/180°C, for 45 minutes, or until golden brown.

4 Meanwhile, put the sugar, honey, and water into a pan and bring to a boil over a low heat, stirring constantly, until the sugar has dissolved completely. Simmer for about 10 minutes, add the lemon juice and simmer for an additional 5 minutes.

5 Using a spatula, carefully transfer the angel hair nests to a serving dish. Pour over the honey syrup, sprinkle over the remaining nuts, and set aside to cool completely before serving. Serve the nests at room temperature with the strained plain yogurt.

german noodle dessert

serves four

4 tbsp butter, plus extra for greasing

6 oz/175 g ribbon egg noodles

½ cup cream cheese

1 cup cottage cheese

scant ½ cup superfine sugar

2 eggs, beaten lightly

½ cup sour cream

1 tsp vanilla extract

pinch of ground cinnamon

1 tsp grated lemon peel

¼ cup slivered almonds

generous ⅓ cup dry white
    bread crumbs

confectioners' sugar, for dusting

1 Lightly grease an oval casserole dish with a little butter. Bring a large pan of water to a boil over a medium heat. Add the noodles and cook for 10 minutes, or until done. Drain thoroughly and set aside.

2 Beat the cream cheese with the cottage cheese, and superfine sugar in a large mixing bowl until the mixture is smooth. Add the beaten eggs, a little at a time, beating thoroughly after each addition.

3 Stir in the sour cream, vanilla extract, cinnamon, and lemon peel, and fold in the noodles. Transfer the mixture to the prepared dish and level the surface.

4 Melt the butter in a small skillet over a low heat. Add the almonds and cook gently, stirring constantly, for about 1–1½ minutes, or until lightly colored. Remove the skillet from the heat and stir the bread crumbs into the almonds.

5 Sprinkle the almond and bread crumb mixture evenly over the top of the dessert and cook in a preheated oven at 350°F/180°C, for about 35–40 minutes until just set. Dust the top with a little sifted confectioners' sugar and serve.

baked sweet ravioli

serves four

SWEET PASTA DOUGH

3¾ cups all-purpose flour

10 tbsp butter, plus extra
    for greasing

¾ cup superfine sugar

4 eggs

1 oz/25 g yeast

½ cup warm milk

FILLING

⅔ cup chestnut paste

½ cup cocoa powder

¼ cup superfine sugar

½ cup chopped almonds

1 cup crushed amaretti cookies

⅝ cup orange marmalade

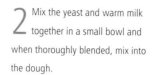

2 Mix the yeast and warm milk together in a small bowl and when thoroughly blended, mix into the dough.

3 Knead the dough for 20 minutes. Cover with a clean dish towel and set aside in a warm place for about 1 hour to rise.

4 Mix the chestnut paste, cocoa powder, sugar, almonds, crushed amaretti cookies, and marmalade together in a separate bowl.

5 Grease a large cookie sheet with a little butter.

6 Lightly flour the counter. Roll out the pasta dough into a thin sheet and cut into 2-inch/5-cm circles with a plain cutter.

1 To make the sweet pasta dough, sift the flour into a bowl, then mix in the butter, sugar, and 3 eggs.

7 Put a spoonful of filling onto each circle, then fold in half, pressing the edges to seal. Arrange on the prepared cookie sheet, spacing the ravioli out well.

8 Beat the remaining egg and brush all over the ravioli to glaze. Cook in a preheated oven at 350°F/180°C, for 20 minutes. Serve hot.

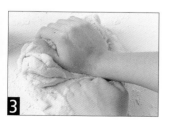

raspberry fusilli

COOK'S TIP

You could use almost any sweet, really ripe berry for making this dessert. Strawberries and blackberries are especially suitable, combined with the correspondingly flavored liqueur. Alternatively, you could use a different berry mixed with the fusilli, but still pour over the raspberry sauce.

1 Bring a large pan of lightly salted water to a boil over a medium heat. Add the pasta and cook until done. Drain thoroughly, then return to the pan and let cool.

2 Using a metal spoon, firmly press 1⅓ cups of the raspberries through a strainer set over a large mixing bowl to form a smooth paste.

3 Put the raspberry paste and sugar into a small pan and simmer over a low heat, stirring occasionally, for 5 minutes. Stir in the lemon juice and set the sauce aside until required.

4 Add the remaining raspberries to the pasta in the pan and mix together well. Transfer the raspberry and pasta mixture to a serving dish.

5 Spread the almonds out onto a cookie sheet and toast under a preheated hot broiler until golden. Remove and let cool slightly.

6 Stir the raspberry liqueur into the reserved raspberry sauce and mix together well until very smooth. Pour the raspberry sauce over the pasta, then generously sprinkle over the toasted almonds and serve.